UP HOME

UP HOME

One Girl's Journey

RUTH J.
SIMMONS

RANDOM HOUSE
NEW YORK

Published in the United States by Random House,
an imprint and division of Penguin Random House LLC, New York.

RANDOM HOUSE and the HOUSE colophon are registered trademarks
of Penguin Random House LLC.

Library of Congress Cataloging-in-Publication Data
Names: Simmons, Ruth, author.
Title: Up home: one girl's journey / by Ruth J. Simmons.
Description: First edition. | New York: Random House, [2023]
Identifiers: LCCN 2023010288 (print) | LCCN 2023010289 (ebook) |
ISBN 9780593446003 (hardcover: acid-free paper) |
ISBN 9780593446010 (ebook)
Subjects: LCSH: Simmons, Ruth | Women college presidents—
United States—Biography. | Women educators—United States—
Biography. | Smith College—History. | Brown University—History. |
Prairie View A&M University—History.
Classification: LCC LA2311 .S56 2023 (print) | LCC LA2311 (ebook) |
DDC 378.0092 [B]—dc23/eng/20230621
LC record available at https://lccn.loc.gov/2023010288
LC ebook record available at https://lccn.loc.gov/2023010289

Printed in the United States of America on acid-free paper

randomhousebooks.com

4 6 8 9 7 5 3

Book design by Susan Turner

*To the extraordinary people who gave me the
strength and means to pursue an unlikely path*

PROLOGUE

I WAS BORN TO BE SOMEONE ELSE. SOMEONE, THAT IS, WHOSE life is defined principally by race, segregation, and poverty. As a young child marked by the sharecropping fate of my parents and the culture that predominated in East Texas in the 1940s and '50s, I initially saw these factors as limiting what I could do and who I could become.

That, in the end, I did not become the person I was born to be still, at times, confuses and perplexes me. Throughout my seventy-plus years, I have been struggling to understand why the early circumstances of my life did not, in the end, define me. I have now come to realize that I have become the person I am today, rather than the person I expected to be, because of the people I knew when I was young—my family, my teachers, my community. They intercepted my modest expectations, boosted my confidence that the future could be different, and sent me on my way with all the support they could muster.

In May 2022, Harvard University, where I earned my

PhD in Romance Languages and Literatures, honored me during a special convocation for the graduating classes of 2020 and 2021, who had missed their commencement ceremonies because of the Covid pandemic health protocols. The ceremony took place on the traditional outdoor commencement site, Tercentenary Theatre. The large space in Harvard Yard is bounded by Memorial Church, Sever Hall, Widener Library, and University Hall. After processing to the covered stage next to Memorial Church, I took my seat in the front row between the honorary degree recipients and the speaker, Attorney General Merrick Garland. Looking out over the scores of crimson-colored university flags and banners and the thousands of joyful celebrants is a heady experience under any circumstance but, on that occasion, I found it especially moving because it brought to mind the perennial question "How did I end up here?"

It was not clear to me why Harvard decided to honor me on that occasion; I had received an honorary degree twenty years earlier, had been invited back as a speaker on many occasions, had been awarded the Centennial Medal there, and had chaired a visiting committee for the Board of Overseers. I did not know, nor had I been advised, how I would be honored. After the presentation of the honorary degrees and immediately before the introduction of the speaker, I was directed to stand for the reading of a citation in my honor. Listening to the president of Harvard, Larry Bacow, speak of my career and accomplishments, I could hardly concentrate on his words; I was musing about the improbability of the moment. Was I really the person animating his generous laudatory remarks?

I looked out over this broad expanse where I spent so many years as a student. I recalled how skeptical some in my department had been, wondering whether I was on a fool's errand there. After all, what was a Black girl to do with a PhD in Romance Languages in 1970s America? Didn't I know that I needed to aim for something more practical and more in tune with the civil rights struggle? I recalled wandering about this very space, heading to class in Sever or going up the majestic steps of Widener to my graduate student carrel. Uncertain of the eventual outcome of my academic efforts, though away from the South, I was still trying to prove my intelligence and worth by showing that I was equal to and perhaps smarter than many of the privileged students studying alongside me. One of my professors later told me that some in the department thought there would be no place for me in the profession I was so keen to pursue.

These recollections washed over me as the president continued to read the citation. Again, I asked myself, "How could I be standing on the stage being celebrated when so many had doubted my ability?" While a student at Harvard, I was evidently not the person I was supposed to be. The incongruity between how my professors viewed me when I studied there and the laudatory citation acknowledging my accomplishments put in sharp focus the improbability of my journey.

This book tries to explain how many people and educational opportunities erased that improbability. From the time I was born in East Texas to my retirement as the first Black president of an Ivy League university, my life has been marked by encounters with extraordinary people. I have not always recognized at the time the unusual character of my experiences, nor have I always been intentional in eschewing what I thought fate might have dictated for my life. Through it all, though, I have come to understand how rich and varied any life can be irrespective of the circumstances thought to dictate a certain path.

I hope that recounting the events and people of my early life will satisfy those who are curious about why my life took the turn that it did. More than that, I hope it will help young people understand that, whatever the circumstances of their lives, they are born not to be the person that history, limited resources, and others dictate but, rather, the person that they are willing to pour their heart and soul into becoming.

PART ONE

East Texas

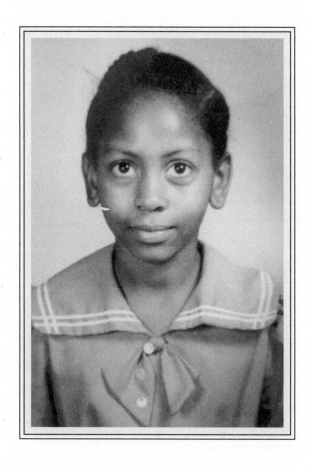

1

Crossroads

I WAS BORN AT A CROSSROADS: A CROSSROADS IN HISTORY, A crossroads in culture, and a geographical crossroads. In North Houston County in East Texas, just a few miles from where the Trinity River separates Houston County from Leon County and the town of Grapeland from Oakwood, is a small community called Daly. The last of my parents' twelve children, I was born there in 1945. Delivered by midwife Addie Bryant in my family's small, dilapidated house, I entered the world near my maternal grandparents' sixty-acre homestead off Texas Highway 227.

The nearest town of any size, where my family could make purchases and transact business, was fifteen miles away and accessible only over dirt roads that could easily wash out during downpours. Going to Grapeland, where there were schools, paved streets, a general store, a bank, and

even a movie theater, would have been tantamount to glam-
orous long-distance travel had it not been for the difficulties
of navigating hilly, unpaved roads in a horse-drawn wagon.
Using this crude mode of transportaion, we would occasionally go "to town" if we could not purchase an essential item
via the Sears catalog. The unsteadiness of the wagon when
crossing creeks on makeshift lumber bridges or struggling to
climb hills on clay subsoils often terrified me. But at the end
of this perilous journey, Grapeland, the first stop in my effort
to learn about the world and the center of all promise,
awaited.

In this small town, we would see people from around the
region who seemed so different from people on the Daly
farms, where my parents were sharecroppers. Dressed in
store-bought clothes instead of rough burlap, walking freely
around the town, and entering establishments through the
front door, whites possessed a freedom and power that were
distant from what we knew, and it was fascinating to observe
them. They were like characters from the fantastical animal
fables my father told us come to life in human form. There
was "Bruh" Rabbit hurrying mischievously about and the sly
fox skulking in doorways, ready to outwit everyone. These
characters fascinated me and made me want to see more of
life than I could see in Daly. My intellectual and cultural
wanderlust began on these infrequent trips to Grapeland, a
town established in the late nineteenth century that became
known as the crossroads of the region. My wanderlust would
grow over time and eventually take me far from East Texas,
first via my imagination and books and, ultimately, in reality.

Grapeland's first name, The Crossroads, reflected its location at the junction of two roads, one that led north from Crockett, the county seat, to Palestine, a commercial center for North Houston County. The other led west from Augusta toward the banks of the Trinity River. When the number of settlers grew and the site needed a more formal name, the town became Grapevine, but the Houston and Great Northern Railroad, which had built a railroad through the town in 1871, renamed it Grapeland, after the area's troublesome and ubiquitous grapevines.

The cheap, rich soil in the Daly area encouraged my maternal grandparents, Richard Campbell and Emma Johnson, to settle there in the 1880s. I am left to imagine what could have impelled the young couple to set off from Mississippi with such a mission, but in the era of their exodus, the Southwest must surely have offered greater safety and opportunity for Blacks. Emma was born after slavery ended officially, and nothing is known of the family members she left in Mississippi, as she never spoke of them. Richard came originally from Virginia. He was born around 1870 to Martha Leonard and Andrew Campbell, both of whom had been slaves. Martha's two boys, Doc and Richard, had different fathers, a fact that was apparent from their features. Doc was very dark with prominent Negroid features, and Richard was very fair with Caucasian features. The Campbell boys gradually worked their way south to Mississippi, where Richard met Emma and the three set off together on a boat for Texas. They landed in Oakwood, an East Texas town founded in 1870 on the Trinity River, across from Daly.

After arriving in Oakwood, Emma and Richard soon made their jump-the-broom marriage legal by remarrying and recording their union in the Leon County courthouse. Their Holy Union of Matrimony took place on August 19, 1891, nine days after they had secured their marriage license, with Reverend Frank Lloyd, an ordained minister, officiating. The same "Minister of the Gospel" officiated when Doc married Bella Tryon, his second wife, two years later. Together, in 1910, Richard and Doc bought sixty acres of farmland situated sixteen miles northwest of Crockett in Daly. The purchase, made jointly with their wives for three hundred dollars, required diligent planning, saving, and no small amount of ambition.

It is easy to see why Richard, Doc, Emma, and Bella crossed the river to farm in tiny Daly, where expansive cotton fields were surrounded by red oak and post oak trees and transected by creeks. Without a town center, the area was home to homesteads large and small that depended on Grapeland and other towns for many needs. The absence of a busy town center gave Daly a quiet, peaceful character in a setting of gently rolling hills and verdant, fertile fields. Even today when I visit the area, I am taken aback by the beauty of the landscape, despite its deteriorating homes and farm buildings and overgrown fields.

The creeks were sites of much childhood enjoyment and religious rituals. Many baptisms took place in them before the churches built baptismal fonts. "When we gather by the river . . . The beautiful, beautiful river . . ." wafted over the congregants when ministers baptized children, submerging them quickly in the water with their noses and mouths covered. Terrified children, dressed in white, momentarily resisted the minister's efforts, but the brief ceremony was over before they could prevent the submersion, no matter how much they struggled. These creeks were also where children gathered outside their parents' sight to swim. Among the few opportunities for sports, the waterways afforded boys the opportunity for swimming, while girls were often discouraged from similar activities. The water could also evoke great fear when it rose during downpours, washing out bridges and spooking horses that were pulling wagons over slippery roads. One particularly terrifying moment of my childhood was having to descend from our wagon so that it could cross a creek without the weight of passengers. Even today, so many years later, I can recall how traumatized I was by that experience.

My mother, Fannie Campbell, was born on this beautiful land in 1906. She met and married my father, Isaac Stubblefield, there and bore all of her children within a few miles of her parents' home. A devoted creature of this intimate landscape, she traveled only to Grapeland, Oakwood, and, occasionally, county fairs in the region. For much of her life, she had only horses and wagons as transport and, after our family acquired an automobile, she never learned to drive. Her marriage also circumscribed her movements; she followed the many relocations prompted by my father's employment first as a farmhand and sharecropper and, later, as a laborer in Houston.

Today, at the point where the paved section of Route 227 abruptly changes into hardened pebbly clay leading toward Cedar Branch, another Grapeland-area community, a meandering climb to the left leads to the top of a cattle-grazed knoll where a small, weather-worn house once looked out over the fields below. With no street addresses, houses and properties often acquired the names of former owners or inhabitants. My father had moved our family to the house previously inhabited by Eddie Bryant, a local farmer, and there I was born after the end of World War II.

I have no personal recollection of the Eddie Bryant house because a couple of years after I was born our family moved to the Murray Farm, working the Murrays' cotton fields. Because I can drive from Grapeland to Daly in only ten or fifteen minutes, the isolation of the Murray Farm and other sites in Daly when I was a child is difficult to imagine today. Yet, in the twenties, thirties, and forties, round-trip travel from the area to Grapeland and back would have taken the better part of a day, making it impossible to go there with any frequency.

The Murray Farm was a village unto itself, with its own convenience store and a sanctified church and school close by. Sharecroppers typically bought on credit from the farm store, where mounting indebtedness to the owners often could not be satisfied. I was too young to be aware of the dire economic factors affecting sharecroppers. Like other families, we had a farm-owned house and a modest amount of space for a garden and chickens. These accommodations met our basic needs. All sharecroppers enjoyed the same state and, having this in common, they generally got along well and built friendships on the basis of their shared circumstances. We were especially close to our nearest neighbors on the farm: Miss Lula May, Miss Florida, and Miss Sis. While I do not recall knowing many sharecroppers, their colorful names continued to live in family lore long after we moved away, perhaps because they typified the proclivity of Blacks to give their children names such as Mr. Son, Baby Girl, Mr. Junior, Mr. Brother, and so on.

The churches in Daly were the primary social outlets for Black sharecroppers. My father's oldest brother, Elmo, helped establish Greater New Hope Baptist Church in the 1920s, just steps away from the Campbell sixty acres on Route 227. The building they erected was a rudimentary structure. The church remains today a center to which people return once a year for "homecoming."

Home going and home coming are important concepts in the South, particularly in Black southern culture. "Going home" could mean going to heaven after death (as in gospel singer Mahalia Jackson's magnificent spiritual in the film *Imitation of Life*), or it could simply mean returning to a country family's ancestral home. Among my family and circle of relatives from Houston County, "up home" is synonymous with Grapeland, but every family defines "up home" on the basis of their town of origin. I suppose if Grapeland had been south of Houston, we would have said "down home." "Down home" also connotes a return to one's roots, to something that is basic, homespun, or a simple evocation of the original spirit of home, as in "down home" music or "down home" eating. I associate "up home" with all of the meanings and nuances of "down home."

Yet in my early years I had no sentimental attachment to this area. I yearned instead for distant, forbidden regions. Aware that some were moving away from the area, I wondered what their lives might become elsewhere. I wondered how moving away might shape my own life. As my older siblings relocated to Houston in search of work, I looked forward to their letters telling of the world beyond the fields that I played in. With no images from television, movies, or magazines available, my imagination was free to build a whimsical world geography and imagine capitals and people unlike any I would later meet. While today's children are stimulated by a barrage of visual and auditory sensations from their very first moment of life, we had nothing of the sort.

Our stimulation came in part from playing with and observing the pets and feral animals on our farm: dogs and cats, birds and reptiles, squirrels and raccoons, horses and deer. Either they manifested unique personalities or we simply attributed exceptional traits to them. My father told us stories that anthropomorphized "coons," squirrels, foxes, deer, and other animals, but we also relied on our own encounters with real animals to keep us amused.

Our home was abuzz with sounds of farm activity, but what I enjoyed most were the many hymns that floated through the house and fields. These could be heard at any time of night or day, and they usually served as accompaniment for the many tasks my mother performed. She typically sang or hummed her favorite songs: "Old Ship of Zion," "Amazing Grace," "Jesus, Keep Me Near the Cross," and many Negro spirituals. Singing was also a favorite pastime for others in the family. My sisters and I formed a trio that performed in church, still much talked about and ridiculed by family members. Recollections of my singing invariably bring gales of laughter.

Other daily activities included traveling dirt roads and exploring fields in our bare feet, harvesting the grapes and prickly bull nettles in the fields, and creating games that my sisters and I played to keep ourselves out of trouble with the older children and my parents. "Pat-a-cake," jumping rope, and hopscotch helped us occupy time on days when we were not in the field or performing household chores.

Initially, Mama and Daddy had horses. We children were generally dependent on our feet when the wagon was hauling cotton and horses were in use pulling plows. Both playmates and adversaries, these horses often entertained us with their remarkable personalities. For sport, Old Dan, Daddy's mean horse, would chase us, slobbering into our hair and tripping us. Mama's horse, Minnie, disliked my father for some reason and she would provoke him. One day my father was beside himself with anger after Minnie chased him onto our porch. In a fury, he retrieved his shotgun from the house and hurried back outside to end Minnie's days. Seeing my father with the gun, the horse loped away into the woods. Our beloved animals were our salvation on the long days when boredom often took hold.

Of course, isolation was sometimes an advantage in the racially segregated and hostile world of 1940s Texas. Encounters with whites often meant danger. The danger of not stepping aside as required when a white person passed. The danger of looking white people directly in the eyes and inexplicably offending them. The danger of speaking impudently or with too much authority. The danger of appearing too proud. The danger of being in the wrong place. The danger of overstepping well-understood boundaries. In the presence of whites, one lived on edge because any of them, no matter their station, could summarily condemn a Black person to injury or punishment. So our parents urged us to observe the proper behavior when encountering whites. And, out of fear, we did.

Racial mixing in a social context was taboo. My eldest brother, Elbert, a responsible and "mannerly" child, was often admired by adults and given special privileges because of his maturity. When invited to a white man's house to hear his daughter play the piano, Elbert considered it a great honor, but once he arrived at the large white house in Grapeland he was told, to his surprise, that he could not go inside; he would have to stand at the side window to listen. This indignity was typical of the behavior of whites in that era. To invite a Black person into one's home or church would suggest social parity, an inconceivable notion.

Interracial activity in Grapeland was filled with such in-dignities. All institutions, of course, were segregated. Sepa-rate churches, separate communities, separate social events, and separate seating were ordained to prevent racial mixing. In the only local movie theater, Blacks were consigned to the balcony. Even places on the streets and sidewalks were ear-marked for one or the other race. After they had made their purchases and dropped their cotton at the local gin, Blacks typically gathered for recreation and socializing in an area on the side of the general store. No restaurants were available to them, so they bought meats and cheese and took their meal to that separate area to eat. Summer sausage and saltines, cheddar cheese, and red "sodie water" were a common meal, with ice cream and candy for children. My favorites were root-beer-flavored barrel candy, coconut striped candy, and peanut butter logs. The gathering site for Blacks was called "buzzards' roost." To many white people in Grapeland, we were a bunch of crude Blacks who reminded them of a flock of buzzards, gathering to feed on leavings and detritus. We swooped in, circled, came down for a feeding, and, once we had our fill, moved on until the next feeding.

Yet racial mixing did occur. Some of the Blacks and whites who passed each other on the streets were blood relatives. We did not acknowledge this fact openly, but in a small town the truth was inescapable. Often family bonds were privately acknowledged as whites visited their Black relatives in the latters' homes and neighborhoods, but never in the white relatives' homes. The evidence of miscegenation was sometimes plain to see in the Black faces that abruptly turned away to avoid being mistaken for "uppity niggers." My father's mother, Flossie Beasley, was related to one of Grapeland's founding families. She was the granddaughter of Liza, a slave, and Jim Beazley, a white man. Even though the spelling of the surname changed, Flossie's fair skin and straight hair, combined with other features, made her ties to the white Beazleys starkly evident. This history was not as well known to us as children, but adults accepted it as a manifestation of the pathos and hypocrisy of racial segregation.

Despite these circumstances, I grew up with little resentment of white privilege. Although my siblings and I set different expectations for ourselves, my parents did not appear to accept more than what was dealt them. Seemingly accepting the fact that they had no power to change their circumstances, they mostly enjoyed their lives in rural East Texas. On my rare forays into Grapeland, I saw the treatment my parents and their friends received. These were my first lessons in the barriers people construct that can so easily denigrate human worth and poison relations between races. At the first opportunity, many of the "buzzards" so mistreated by the town would leave Grapeland, taking with them to new lives a large measure of the humiliation that had been inflicted upon them during their time in this Crossroads of Houston County.

To be born in an environment in which one is legally designated subhuman is a defining experience. Constant assertions that one is less deserving of basic human and civil rights can become deeply ingrained, dominating one's self-image and blocking the will to pursue ambitious goals or express one's true identity. I have frequently been told by whites that Blacks have "a chip on their shoulder." They often say this as if it is ridiculous to have been marked deeply by the violation of one's human dignity and rights. It is true that ideally we should not permit even the most heinous circumstances to mar permanently the course of our thinking and our lives, but we should not forget that such an ideal is more a desirable goal than an easy accomplishment. Living one's life during and after the violation of one's humanity is a test and task that any would find challenging, and it can be, at the least, an arduous lifelong pursuit.

Although I did not by any means witness firsthand the worst of what my parents and the rest of my family experienced in Grapeland, I was certainly made aware that being Black enclosed me in a web of stereotypes which I would not likely escape. I had no thought that I would be exempt from the treatment my parents recounted from their past. To avoid being overtaken by the circumstances I had inherited, I had to imagine the world as a far more interesting and logical place, much as one might stubbornly build a castle in the sand, knowing that it will be washed away. But I never expected my imagined castles to replace permanently the reality of rural East Texas in the forties and fifties.

Today, I own the land that my mother inherited from her mother. Once married, Mama never again lived on this land; she followed the moves and inhabited the homes dictated by my father's employment. Though undeveloped, this land is worth my owning because it represents the strivings of the Campbells and Stubblefields and the deep and willful connections that Mama and Daddy made to each other and the region. I return to the red clay roads and sandy fields of Daly as often as I can to remind myself what I learned there: the need to stretch beyond the boundaries imposed upon me as a child. I return to marvel at how my interest in far different worlds was kindled as I wandered barefoot through the fields and meadows. I return to contemplate what my grandparents Emma and Richard, and my mother and father must have endured to keep us safe and to instill in us a sense of self-worth in the face of colossal barriers to pride and accomplishment. And so, I hold on to this land because "up home" is a journey I will always make and "down home" is a feeling I will always relish.

2

Miss Fannie and Mr. Ike

ONE OF MY EARLIEST MEMORIES IS OF MY MOTHER sobbing as she read a letter from my brother Wilford. Wilford, Mama's third child, left home in 1947 to join my oldest brother, Elbert, and seek work in Houston. He found a job initially as a day laborer but enlisted in the army in 1948 for a three-year tour of duty. His motivation for enlisting was to earn steady pay that he could send to my parents in Grapeland. Even at a young age, Wilford was family-centered, loyal, obedient, and generous. Generosity in the ubiquitously impoverished world we knew marked him as unusual. His good nature, however, made him the object of teasing and bullying by family members and peers. Identified early on as Mama's favorite, he enjoyed her protection as well as that of my older sisters and brothers when they saw others outside the family bullying him. Quick to cry in deep, mournful howls, he remained the butt of derision for much of his time in Grapeland and even beyond. But he was deeply loved and respected by everyone in the family.

The sight of my mother sobbing aroused in me the deepest feelings of uncertainty and insecurity. I searched her face to understand what she was feeling. She stood on the creaky, leaning front porch of our paint-starved house as she continued to look down at the letter. I eventually understood that Wilford's letter had brought news of his deployment to Korea. Too young to understand the implications of this conflict in a distant country, I cared only that this news had brought Mama, the strongest person I knew, to tears.

Her tears no doubt reflected her sadness that this child whom she had protected from childhood tormentors would have to defend himself in a war. Perhaps she was also fearful that her gentle son would not have the heart to protect himself if it meant taking another person's life. I pulled on her housedress to learn what was happening, but she ignored me. Even in the face of my evident distress, she did not respond.

Uncertainty and fear, though rare in my own consciousness at that point in my life, were all too familiar to my mother. By the time I was born, she had known many hardships. I wonder if she recalled a moment when she looked to her mother with the same apprehension I felt that day. Her mother, Emma Johnson, born during Reconstruction, had weathered the challenges of African American life following slavery. The death of her husband Richard left her to rear six young children in the harsh and desperate first decades of the twentieth century. In spite of that, she kept her children close, provided for them, and maintained a useful and involved life that was, in spite of her nineteenth-century clothes and manners, modern in numerous ways. Long before women were accorded that right, Emma declared herself an independent woman, charting her own course and determined to live her life on her own terms. To reassure one's children in the face of one's own fear and uncertainty is one of the most demanding but empowering acts of motherhood. Emma provided that for her children, and my mother, Fannie, did the same for my siblings and me. But on the day that Wilford's letter arrived, Fannie forgot to hide her fear and, as a consequence, my own was born.

As the last of twelve children, I was the beneficiary of much attention. Until that moment, it had not occurred to me that anything terrible could happen to me. My father, mother, and all my brothers and sisters would have protected me, I thought, from any adverse circumstances. Only vaguely conscious of the perilous daily reality for Blacks, I felt secure in the fact that I was shielded by a phalanx of family members who would prevent any harm to me.

At that time, my family was eking out a substandard living on the Murray Farm, which provided cotton to support growing consumer demand for textiles following World War II. Cotton was an especially challenging crop, demanding a large number of workers. Our family—parents and children—worked for a series of plantation owners as sharecroppers. On these farms, we always lived in owner-provided housing that, had there been any government housing codes, would have missed the required safety standards by a wide margin. Small, poorly built clapboard constructions with corrugated tin roofs and without upkeep or routine maintenance made up the typical housing inventory on such farms.

Our house on the Murray Farm was little more than a shanty. Set on wooden blocks, it was a cube of weathered wood with a tin roof. Behind a front room was a kitchen with a wood-burning stove. There were two bedrooms, one for boys and one for girls, with my parents sleeping in the front room, which doubled as a sitting room during the day. There was little need for chairs and a sofa inside, and that was fortunate, since we didn't have a sofa. The kitchen was where we prepared and ate our meager meals of cornbread and pork-seasoned peas and beans and sought warmth beside a woodstove in the colder months. It was also a place for Saturday night baths in a large tin tub. Moving brought no relief from this essential pattern, as all of the houses we lived in had the same features and limitations.

Under the sharecropping system, it was difficult—most of the time, impossible—to accumulate assets of one's own; owners extended credit for essentials, and the resulting debt was often difficult to repay. From year to year, ours was subsistence living at best. Yet in spite of this harsh environment, I had what I thought at the time was a comfortable childhood, nestled in the bounty of my family's care. The memory of my mother's tears that day stands out because I had until that moment felt so secure. I have revisited this scene often during my adult life because of what my brother Wilford later came to mean to me.

Having grown up working in the fields and earning very little as the sharecropping era was drawing to a close, my oldest brothers left home to seek employment in Houston. Elbert was the first to go. The oldest child, he was in many ways the model for everyone else in the family. Tall, handsome, and mature beyond his years, he possessed a pacific attitude that was the antithesis of what the cruel farming environment should have produced. He married Erma Mae Hicks, whose family lived a short distance from our home, and after a year, they moved to Houston.

There was tension between the Hicks and Stubblefield families. Some accused the matriarch of the Hicks family, Miss Rosa Lee, of being haughty and contemptuous of the Stubblefields. Her more amiable husband, Mr. Hubbard (so called, although his name was Herbert), was a wiry, complacent man who was fair with Caucasian features. Their daughter Erma Mae was light brown with straight hair, and her twin, Herman, was dark-skinned. There was also some suspicion in our family toward Erma because frankly, some hinted, she shared Miss Rosa Lee's disdain for the Stubblefields. Erma's indomitable independence gave her an air of arrogance and fueled her efforts to achieve social and economic advancement. Though she proved herself a loving wife, her drive to advance personally tended to govern her judgment of (and, often, contempt for) those who did not share her aspirations to the middle class.

Elbert and Erma were an example to others in my family that, through planning, ambition, and sacrifice, former sharecroppers who moved to the city could manage and even overcome the social and economic problems that had afflicted them. Once they moved away, their letters sustained us through the years of separation (we didn't have a telephone). Often they urged my parents to move to Houston and sent money to help the family left behind on the farm.

Chester, the second of my seven brothers, had also moved to Houston. He had had a troubled relationship with my father. I am told that one day, at the age of sixteen, after a particularly severe beating by my father, he left home for good. Houston was just close enough to Grapeland that children reaching their late teens or adulthood could imagine trying to make a life on their own there, especially when, by the late 1940s, plenty of relatives had already proven that life in the city was much easier than toiling in the fields of our isolated community.

Elbert, Chester, Wilford. That was the order of their birth, each coming a year and a half apart. Elbert was the staunchly mature aide-de-camp for my mother as she tried to raise the rest of us. More like a parent than a brother, he commanded respect from the younger children, and his directives, like those of my parents, were not to be questioned. My mother placed great confidence in him. Chester was the perennially misbehaving middle child of this triumvirate. The shortest in stature and the son who most resembled my father, he was stubborn, but he was my mother's protector and defender. I don't know what it was about my mother that so endeared her to her sons. Her daughters were faithful as well, but her sons especially so. I have sometimes thought that her bond with them and their respect for her had something to do with the fact that my father was unable or unwilling to form close relationships with any of his boys.

When Wilford was born, my mother was accustomed to babies. Still, he was apparently from the very start especially dear to her. Unlike strong Elbert and bellicose Chester, Wilford had a sensitive nature. Called "Red" because of his ruddy skin color, he tended to avoid the intense daily intersibling mischief and rivalry but was nevertheless the constant butt of pranks. My oldest sister, Atherine, born seventeen months after Wilford, was his chief tormentor in the family but also his chief defender in schoolyard skirmishes. She would take on the strongest boy who bullied Wilford or any of the other children.

Elbert, Chester, Wilford, and Atherine constituted the senior cohort among the children. Albert, Arnold, and Nora were the middle cohort, and Ruben, Clarence, the twins (Azella and Ozella), and I were the last. The oldest were parental figures who shouldered most of the immense burden of the harsh farming life. From early ages, they labored long hours in the fields in searing heat and pushed plows to prepare hard ground for planting. Without shoes to protect them from the biting sand and painful pebbles underfoot, they suffered many cuts and punctures that Mama treated with kerosene. Frequently, they ate no more than a couple of biscuits before starting the day. With the demands of sharecropping, daily school attendance was out of the question, and most of the first cohort dropped out of high school before graduating. So Wilford's choices, and those of the other older children, were limited as they set out to find a life in Houston.

After enlisting in the army, Wilford had the good fortune of two delays in being sent into combat. Not having had proper oral care in Grapeland, he needed dental work that prevented him from departing with his all-Black regiment, many of whom were killed. Once he was shipped off to Japan in preparation for a Korean landing, he injured his hand playing basketball and again was held back until his injury healed.

The picture of him as a young man in his army uniform, one of my mother's favorites, is one of the few photographs we have of one of our older siblings as teens or young adults. Seeing that photograph and knowing his nature, I understand why my mother was so fearful for him as a soldier.

In the months that followed that moment when I saw Mama crying, I frequently thought about how my life might change unexpectedly and, over the next months, I started to pepper my mother with questions. Would she and Daddy always be there? Would my other sisters and brothers leave as Wilford, Chester, and Elbert had done? Would I see them again? Would I ever die? As a contented child, I had been immune to anxiety; yet on the day that I began to understand Mama's fears for her children, my worries commenced, and they remained with me for most of my youth. Much later, I came to understand better the true nature of my mother's strength, but images of her vulnerability dominated these childhood years.

My mother has remained somewhat of a puzzle to me. What must it have meant to be born Fannie Eula Campbell in 1906 in East Texas? She spoke of her parents as the dominant influence of her life; their story bespeaks the values she imparted to her own children. Richard Campbell and Emma Johnson were rooted in what they had experienced from slave parents. Emma, up to her death in 1947, followed many of the practices and habits her family had acquired and preserved during slavery. She dressed like a slave for all of her seventy-five years, wearing long dresses made of bleached cotton canvas with an African headdress of similar fabric. She wore plain white cotton dresses during the week and striped cotton dresses on Sundays. Like most at that time, Mama Emma (which we elided to "Mamemma") had only one pair of shoes: black high-top work boots with laces. She was not a large woman, but her heavy petticoats gave the impression that her slight figure was bulkier. In spite of her diminutive size, people invariably remarked on her strength, especially her ability to carry large, heavy loads on her head after the style of African women. She frequently carried water from the well with a full bucket on her head and one in each hand.

Emma had an unusual way of expressing herself. "Thee better get thee biskit on that stump!" she would say to grandchildren who misbehaved. A woman of imposing and, some would say, fierce mien, she was also a memorable disciplinarian. She would direct the miscreants to a small tree stump that provided child-size seating on her front porch. She and my grandfather Richard must have struck quite a picture together; she, with jet-black skin, wearing stark white clothing and a headdress, and he, tall, handsome, and extremely fair.

When Richard died, the land he and Doc had purchased provided the only means for Mamemma to take care of and protect her family. Emma eventually remarried, but her new husband declined to work in the fields. Emma, who couldn't bear to see her children laboring while their stepfather did nothing, confronted him. "The children are in the fields and thee is in the house sleeping. Get thee things and get out!" she ordered. She never married again. Keeping the homestead going with animals to tend and fields to plant was a challenge. Her three daughters and son (Fannie, Aggie, Eliza, and John) were responsible for much of the labor. A daughter, Jim, had died in early adulthood and a son, Richard, had been shot in the kneecap at the age of sixteen while hunting with a cousin and did not survive. Emma managed to see the remaining children live to adulthood. When they married and had families, they settled not far from the Campbell homestead, and Emma's grandchildren became fixtures in her house. Too young when she died, I did not have the pleasure of being consigned to her tree stump for misbehavior.

Richard Campbell's patrician and loving nature and Mamemma's strength and independence helped mold my mother's spirit. Mama was quiet, reflective, kind, generous, and forgiving. The turmoil of a twelve-child household did not seem to faze her. Nor did the need to rise at 4:00 A.M. to prepare for a day of cooking, cleaning, and working in the fields. I often thought that she settled for too little in her life; she voiced no complaints except those pertaining to our misbehavior. She cared little for her appearance and seemed satisfied to comb her hair or fix her braids without fuss and to wear crude and sometimes tattered dresses that no vain woman would don. Deeply religious and attentive to following the Bible's teachings, Mama saw her life as having a specific purpose. Of overriding importance was seeing her children taught the right values and ensuring that they lived to adulthood. But her life was to be considerably more complicated than these simple goals she set for herself.

She met and married my father, Isaac Henry Stubblefield, when she was eighteen. Called "Ike," Daddy was born on August 5, 1904, two years before Fannie. They were married on February 2, 1924, by Reverend Gilford, an AME minister. Their marriage certificate listed Daddy by his nickname

"Ike," and Fannie Eula is entered on the certificate as "Fannie Mae." Fannie was mature beyond her years. She needed to be. She had married a young man who had suffered an even more difficult childhood than she; and, in many ways, he would never recover from the deep scars it had left.

Isaac's parents, Wesley Stubblefield and Flossie Beasley (spelled Beazley on their marriage license) were married in 1898. Little is known about their life together before Wes died prematurely, leaving Flossie with five small children. Elmo, the oldest, was born in 1899, Pete in 1900, Spencer in 1901, Isaac in 1904, and Herbert in 1905. A daughter, Ozella, did not survive beyond infancy. With no means of supporting the children, Flossie quickly remarried. Her new husband turned Wes's children out to fend for themselves. Under the guidance of Elmo, who was barely ten at the time, the abandoned children lived a barren, sometimes homeless life, scrounging for work and food to keep themselves alive. My father's memories of hunger and deprivation during that period marked his outlook and expectations for the rest of his days. He told us he was once so hungry that he retrieved a maggot-infested raccoon carcass for a meal. As a child, I knew little of these harsh details, so I marveled at how satisfied he was with his modest state in life. However limited his life appeared to me, it was a significant improvement over what he had known as a child.

Daddy commanded obedience from all of us, including my mother, with a temper of noisily mammoth scale. He could become angry when food was not prepared to his taste, when chores were not done, when he received "sass" from a child, or when we committed any number of other peccadilloes. Yet when he was not angry, he had the most robust laugh of any person I have ever known. It was not just head bending and shoulder shaking, it engulfed his entire body, feeding on itself, gathering strength until, exhausted, he gave a disbelieving shake of his head and exclaimed, "Ah, lawdy!" He was often laughing at his own stories, for he enjoyed tall tales, true-to-life tales, and mystery tales. His favorite genre was the fable, and these he told repeatedly, embellishing each with new details as the occasion required. We heard often about what "Bruh Rabbit" had said, done, or seen.

To have Daddy and his three brothers all together was to experience an astonishing laugh track. They reached back into their melancholy childhood to find shared memories that, while not discernibly humorous to anyone else listening, threw them into communal fits of hilarity. My sisters and brothers have taken up this very habit, and at any reunion they will recount stories from our childhood, especially about Daddy, that will send us into similar fits of laughter.

Often, our recollections are about the names that Daddy gave each of us. Each name was mildly pejorative, ridiculing most notably our physical features. Elbert was "hickory-nut head"; Wilford, "leather-ears"; and Atherine, "perch-mouth." Fish seemed to be a particularly fertile source of nicknames. Albert was "gar-mouth." Eyes were also a focal point for derision: Clarence was "knob-eyes," while I was "big-eyes." My sister Ozella was "hatchet-face"; Nora, "big-mouth"; and Azella, first "cat-faced" and later "gimley-legged." When we were young, we hated these names, but today, we laugh at them because they so aptly capture our distinguishing features.

My father also used colorful expressions to avoid recognizable obscenities, but we children were never to use obscenities or language that was even marginally offensive. His most common term for a person who transgressed was "jackstropper." This he heaped on anyone and everyone, from the mail carrier who groped my sister to the peddler whose prices were too high. We understood that "jackstropper" denoted a person unworthy of consideration or respect. "Datblamit!" was a substitute for all words connoting "shucks!" He substituted "datblame" or "datblamit" for "goddamn." Variations on "datblame" were "datgum" or "datgummed." "Datbobbit" was also synonymous with "datblamit." We children thought this obscenity avoidance was absurd.

Daddy took care to avoid unambiguous blasphemy because he was studying for the ministry and wanted to steer clear of language that could besmirch his reputation as a minister. In the Black Baptist tradition, one is called to ministry. I never heard precisely when my father "was called," although such an event is usually so significant that the moment is recounted with pride. Often preachers describe this event from the pulpit as a means of showing how their own lives have been transformed by faith and God's choosing. When my mother and father married, they exchanged Bibles as gifts. My father's is full of marginalia in his nearly illegible handwriting. With an eighth-grade education, he read haltingly even in later life. It must have taken a heroic effort to study the Bible and to prove himself worthy of the ministry, which he accomplished after many years.

Daddy was especially fastidious about his person, and he required more bathroom and mirror time than anyone else in our household. He brushed his teeth with great attention, tended his balding head with excited concentration, and chose his clothes with unusual care. I suppose his preening made up for some of the shame he felt as a child when his family was destitute and his mother rejected him and his brothers for a new husband.

As a child, before I came to understand his weaknesses and limitations, my relationship with my father was easy. Being the youngest, I was his favorite and escaped much of the harsh treatment that my brothers, sisters, and mother experienced. Daddy generally gave me wide latitude for mistakes and did not punish me when I got into fights with my sisters or talked back to him. The fact that he spoiled me made me a target for my three youngest sisters: Nora and the twins, Azella and Ozella. Whenever he spared me, they inflicted their special punishment on me, which included pummeling me while calling out my offenses. Occasionally, their doing so meant a scolding because I would report their mistreatment to my father.

My father stood just a bit taller than five feet, which, combined with his volatility, made him want to challenge anyone over the slightest insult to him or his family. Once, Daddy was upset when he heard that a man said he had big eyes. Taking his gun and threatening to reduce his slanderer to nothing, he found the man and called him out for a showdown. "I heard you said that I have big eyes," he yelled. Not budging an inch, the man responded, "I did, Ike. You do have big eyes." My father's only response was to reply sheepishly, "Oh, I just wanted to know if it was true." I don't recall any instance in which he actually followed up on his threats, but many of those who weren't aware of this pattern cowered in the face of them. We think of his cursing with ridiculous substitutes and laugh. We think of his preening and we hoot. We remember his tall tales and his ridiculous cowboy behavior, and we double over with laughter. He gave us that laughter and our intense propensity to find the humor in impossible situations.

It was many years before I became aware of the difficulties of my parents' marriage. As a child I could see my mother's devotion to Daddy in the way that she slavishly waited on him, forbade us from saying anything negative about him, and delighted in his presence. When he wanted something, she would fetch it. If he was displeased with the way something had been done, she would hasten to correct it. She was guided by what my father wanted in every aspect of her life. She was a homemaker who managed the household, served my father, and reared her children with no care for what people outside her family thought of her. We adored her goodness and selflessness, but we did not want to be like her. My father did not act like a caring husband who appreciated my mother's love and sacrifices, and we all, especially the girls, hated her subservience to such an undeserving man. Although we loved our father, we recognized his faults. I don't know if Mama ever saw them.

By the time I was born, they had been married twenty years. My mother had survived my father's beatings, the separations, the quarrels, and the other women. The older brothers and sisters were acutely aware of my father's cruelty and indiscretions, but we younger children were lucky to have missed that stage in our parents' relationship. I had a love for

my father that was for many years free of any real resentment, scorn, or anger. Those things would come into full
bloom later, when I was a teenager, after my mother's death.

During her thirty-seven years of marriage, my mother had
fourteen pregnancies and twelve children who lived beyond
infancy. Our large family, no doubt the source of some of the
difficulties she and my father faced, was also the source of
much of Mama's quiet strength. A large brood of children
was important to farming families. Child labor laws did not
reach Grapeland; children did heavy labor from sunup to
sundown like grown-ups as soon as they were able. The same
pattern of shared effort continued at home.

For most of the year, everyone in the house was up and
on their way to the fields at sunrise. When we returned, there
was only time to wash our feet, eat dinner, and go to bed. We
took turns retrieving water from a well and keeping the
wooden bucket on the porch filled with a dipper for drinking.
There was no electricity or tap water in any of our Daly houses.
When the weather permitted, we spent most of the day outside: chopping wood, feeding animals, sitting on the porch,
or sweeping the dirt in the yard to remove loose dirt, animal
leavings, and debris. We repeatedly swept inside the house to
keep it free of the dirt and dust carried in from the yard and
through the openings in the walls and door. In the winter
months, these cracks brought a damp chill into the largely
unheated house. Mama's quilts kept us warm, and her quilt
making was an important skill, for these houses had no insu-
lation or means of distributing heat from the stove.

Her quilt making was the only art in her life. I would
watch her as she cut the cloth from flour sacks, old clothing,

or fabric remnants into squares or triangles. Matching the pieces, trying different color combinations, and hand-stitching them together, she would slowly assemble a covering large enough for a bed. Then she would attach cotton batting to the back and add a lining. Spreading the lined and stuffed patchwork across two wooden carpentry "horses," she would attach the layers to one another by tacking or stitching them in a predetermined pattern. We loved these quilts not so much because of their undeniable artistry but because Mama had spent so much time bringing them into being, often without a sewing machine.

The porch, an important extension of the house and a preferred workplace for chores, was also a good place for quilting and other activities. This open space was, in effect, the living room that these small shacks lacked. My mother would peel potatoes, shell peas and beans, sew, quilt, and perform a host of other culinary and household tasks there. Without an indoor toilet, the porch was also the place where we washed our hands and faces in shallow enamel-coated basins that hung from nails when not in use. We gathered on the porch to talk or pass the time in rare moments when all the work was done. Children sat on the floor in front of our mother or older sisters to get our hair combed or braided. We also received visitors on the porch. On the day that I watched my mother weeping while reading Wilford's letter, no visitors came, and no chores took place on the porch.

After I became president of Smith College, historic Ewha Womans University in Seoul, Korea, invited me to visit. Over the years growing up and starting my career, my mother's tears for Wilford had been a leitmotif that replayed in my memory. While I was on the airplane to Seoul, suddenly the recollection of my mother on the porch reading Wilford's letter returned. A decade after that day, in 1958, she would die, and her death would further shape my outlook, my sense of self, my values, and my demons. Wilford, safely back from Korea, would become a surrogate parent, my unflagging support through high school and college. Did that letter have anything to do with how I came to rely on him? As I walked through the streets of Seoul, I thought back to the peaceful young boy from Grapeland and how much he sacrificed to send money home to us. I thought of how his life and mine had been shaped by Korea and how different my life would have been if he had been killed there with the rest of his regiment. The thought took my breath away. I finally understood my mother's tears and I couldn't help but cry.

3

_____

Greater New Hope

IN DALY, FAMILY LIFE WAS INDISTINGUISHABLE FROM WORK life; to live was to work from before dawn until the last light of day. On weekdays, my mother washed, ironed, and prepared meals, and we all walked to the fields for whatever work (plowing, hoeing, picking cotton) was to be prioritized that day. Family meals were memorable for what they lacked: barely enough for all of us. Yet I loved those mealtimes because they were my proof of being part of a close, loving family. Together, we shared an experience that we all understood to be unjust. Together, we accepted the fact that the sharecropping conditions were stifling of who we could be. Yet, too young to experience the full measure of these harsh conditions, I experienced my small and secure life as one of relative ease. Surrounded every waking moment by my family, I was a contented child.

When my family performed grueling work such as picking cotton, I escaped the worst of being in the fields. My older siblings placed the cotton bolls picked from the plants into sacks they dragged between the rows of cotton. These eight-foot-long canvas bags, sewn by my mother, were sturdy enough to carry me along with the fluffy bolls stuffed inside. Dragging me along on the end of the bag was difficult, but with every hand including my mother in the field, my youngest sisters and I had to be there too. As soon as children were old enough to handle a smaller version of the adult-size sack and to fill it with cotton picked cleanly—without leaves, seeds, or other debris—they would graduate to being field hands. For most of us, the apprenticeship for cotton picking began around the age of six.

I am told that I was a noisy and curious child, always laughing. Faced with my unconstrained antics, neither my brothers nor my sisters seemed to care what happened to me when I was in their charge. Understandably, with space and resources already so strained, a twelfth child had not been welcome. Yet I was not bothered by their grudging tolerance. My father made up for their resentment; he seemed gloriously happy with me. I was his baby daughter. He delighted in my every antic, laughing easily at whatever I did to annoy others. I later learned that my father treated every youngest child in a similar fashion but, being the last, I never graduated from his preferential treatment.

Being the "baby" of the family was a distressingly permanent condition. Irrespective of my age, strangers, relatives, and frequent visitors asked about "the baby." Often, as if peering into a cradle, they would stare closely at my features and laugh knowingly at how I resembled my parents. "Ike, is *this* your baby girl?" Daddy would bend over backward as the cackle rose from his throat to affirm that I was indeed his baby girl. The youngest of my brothers, Clarence, was just the baby boy. Daddy's memory of his only sister, Ozella, who had died young, and the fact that he had seven sons by the time I was born, might explain why being the baby girl trumped being the baby boy in such a patriarchal family.

In spite of the discomfort I felt about being referred to as "the baby" no matter how old I grew, I had more attention, more candy when my parents went to town, less work than the others, and more forgiveness for my behavior. This status also meant that those outside the family focused attention on me, knowing that their doing so would please my parents. Pleasing my father was easy. Pleasing my mother required some mysterious combination of qualities, such as decency, common sense, and generosity. When she pronounced that a person lacked common sense, it was a harsh indictment, suggesting that they were too ignorant to gain even the most basic understanding of how to treat others and manage day-to-day affairs.

Mama tended to be cautious about outsiders. Some of this caution was due to the isolation of our home, but a great deal was the result of Mama's conviction that nothing was to be gained by visiting with people, especially strangers. Although she was generous in thought and deed, when she had to interact with strangers, she was inclined to distrust them. She was especially careful not to make the mistakes that she thought too many people unthinkingly inflicted upon others. Inexplicably concluding that visiting acquaintances must be an inconvenience, she repeatedly asserted that it was inappropriate to "sit up at people's houses," encumbering their time when they doubtless had much to do. We could wander all over the back roads and fields of our Daly community, swim in the creeks, and plunder the fields without adult supervision, but if my mother heard that we had visited anyone in their homes, she would have our hide. Even when we visited relatives, she would forbid us to accept food offered us because, she thought, they might need it. Yet when anyone visited us, she insisted on offering them our food, making us do without, if necessary. Her kindness left us confused and dismayed that with so little food to spare she would so easily give it away.

Disobeying Mama and Daddy meant a whipping, but defying them in their absence was especially serious. If they said we should remain at home while they were away, any hint that we had gone out would incur serious punishment, generally a sound "whuppin." Whipping generally took the form of a beating with a "switch," a thin tree branch with the leaves removed. The smaller and greener the switch the more it stung our bare legs and arms. For minor infractions, Mama would "maul" our heads. Making a fist, she would hold it against our head, rotating it as if trying to tunnel into our cranium. She delivered these punishments with a lecture reminding us that we'd been treated fairly and given ample warning. Insisting that we find the switch with which we would be lashed was another way of instilling lasting fear and curtailing repeated misbehavior.

As painful as they were, whippings could not compare with the fierce physical fights we children had among ourselves. While our parents were away, we fought protractedly, being careful not to inflict visible damage. From time to time, we failed to keep these fights secret, particularly when we used common household objects big or small to even the balance in the fight of a younger or weaker sibling against an older, stronger one. On one occasion, my sister Atherine threw hot cornbread on Clarence. Others heaved heavier objects, such as an iron or a skillet. This warfare required a deft touch. Evidence that we had harmed one of our siblings in a fight would also bring a beating from our parents.

Each of us had a primary adversary in the family and several secondary ones. My chief antagonists were my fraternal twin sisters, Azella and Ozella, but, until I was much older, they were mostly concerned with their own rivalry. They looked nothing alike and shared no personality traits. Azella was small, tough, and mean. Ozella was larger, slow, and passive. From the time they were toddlers, Azella had given her twin drubbings at regular intervals, bringing my father to Ozella's rescue and singling out "cat-faced" Azella for her meanness. Thanks to their preoccupation with each other, most of the time I was able to keep my distance from the infighting and parental punishment. To escape these squabbles, I looked forward to any opportunity to see people from outside the family circle. Sunday church services afforded such occasions.

The naming of Black churches often involved superlatives that suggested a future better than the present. Resurrection and rebirth imagery added to the idea that our harsh and unjust circumstances would improve. Our family church represented the hope of Black farming families awaiting relief from the trials of segregation and the punishing physical labor that only enriched others. What better name for the church they established than Greater New Hope?

There were a number of churches in the Daly and nearby Cedar Branch area as well as a small one near the Murray Farm, but Greater New Hope was considered our "home church." Mama, reared Methodist like her mother, worshipped with my father and the rest of the family at Greater New Hope, which Uncle Elmo, the venerated eldest of Daddy's brothers, had helped found on Route 227, just up the road from Mamemma's homestead. On Sundays, we would see our uncles, aunts, and cousins there as well as other Black families from all around the Daly community.

Greater New Hope was a modest white wooden structure. In the sanctuary, on either side of the aisle were crude wooden pews made of two wide planks that dipped toward each other in the center, leaving a gap that had a tendency to pinch when one sat. At the end of each pew was an elbow-high armrest that must have been purposefully designed for discomfort. A small choir area was located behind the pulpit. There was just enough room between the pulpit and the front pew for the deacon's table, which held collection plates for tithing and contributions. An important part of the service was the collections march, when row by row worshippers stood and processed to the accompaniment of a triumphal or mournful spiritual; they marched to the deacon's table to deposit their contributions into the plates. Carrying my five cents gave me a brief respite from the uncomfortable pews and a chance to get a good look at everyone in attendance.

Next to the church was a grove of handsome hickory

trees, whose generous canopy bestowed relief from the Texas sun. In the summer, we all tethered our horses, stationed our wagons, or parked our cars under these trees. During annual homecoming events, farm families gathered for a special service followed by a picnic on the lawn. These were lavish affairs, as every family competed to donate the most distinctive dishes. Fried chicken was always plentiful, as were turkey and dressings (always plural), potato salad, and a variety of barbecue, including barbecued goat from time to time, and an array of pies and cakes. The understated but elegant pound cake was my favorite because its taste was never predictable. The six ingredients (flour, milk, butter, sugar, baking powder, and flavoring) tasted subtly different in the hands of different cooks. This version had a touch more vanilla flavoring; that one a richer butter flavor; another a slight almond taste.

Men prepared immense barrels of Kool-Aid, sweetened beyond reason and stirred by whichever father had an arm long enough to reach deep into the barrel and mix the concoction until the sugar disappeared. I loved how the almost always red Kool-Aid flowed generously into my outstretched cup. Although there were many enticing dishes together in this location and so easily within reach, we could eat only food from families that had been cleared by my mother. It wasn't evident what these "good" families had done to get on my mother's food list. Was it their common sense? I wondered. For the most part, members of the Stubblefield or Campbell clans got clearance simply by being related to us. Others somehow managed to secure Fannie's seal of approval because they were upstanding, God-fearing, decent people.

It was not clear why such people produced cleaner, safer, or tastier food.

Because I was the baby of the family, people often brought me special treats, such as tea cakes and, surprisingly, my mother permitted this from select people. However, early on, people thought I was partial to another particular delicacy: chicken feet. In our large family, every part of the chicken was cooked and, since I was the smallest, I was given the feet. One day, apparently hungry, I started crying during the church service and screamed that I wanted chicken feet. From that day on, Miss Mary Isidore dutifully brought me fried chicken feet each Sunday and I became thereafter the little girl who loved chicken feet.

Music was the highlight of church services. My older brothers formed "quartets" and sang spirituals at church and around the region. Elbert was a particularly good singer, and whenever he returned to church on a visit home, I was proud and eager to hear his beautiful solos. His selections were gospel standards and the hymns that we heard in church, and while his untrained voice had a hint of a twang, his natural and sincere delivery greatly affected listeners. Very devout, he didn't try to impress others; he seemed, in a way, to be singing for himself. He, too, was later called to the ministry, and his songs early on reflected that spiritual dedication.

My father, who couldn't "sing a lick," decided to form a trio made up of the youngest of us girls, and my sisters and I sang at church events. We became well known for one song, "Talk About Jesus," where I sang the bass chorus. Azella, with the best voice, led off and, at the chorus, I reached as deep as I could, singing:

Now let us talk, talk, talk
(about Jesus)
Talk, talk, talk
(about Jesus)
Talk, talk, talk
(about Jesus)
Because he's been so good to me.

I would sing the word "talk," sounding each subsequent note in a deeper and deeper voice and opening my already large eyes wider. My performance would provoke a good deal of laughter and applause. These were the first times I recall singing in front of an audience. I was aware that I did not have a beautiful voice, but the pleasure people took in hearing me struggle with the bass was satisfying. As one who was often seen by family members as a nuisance, I found this affirmation encouraging.

Recitations were another type of our church performances. We had to memorize and recite biblical passages (the Beatitudes were my favorite assignment), and we would deliver viva voce poems such as James Weldon Johnson's "Creation," with utmost intensity and stiffly contrived gestures. Leading up to the day of our performance, we would practice faithfully so that we would not forget our lines.

We were accustomed to Bible passages as Mama and Daddy encouraged memorized verses at home. At the end of the blessing before each meal, each of us would have to utter a brief verse from the Bible. Doing so was the equivalent of "Amen" following the saying of grace. Most of the time, for brevity and in breathless anticipation of the hot meal that awaited, some of us simply said "Jesus wept," the shortest verse in the Bible. Anyone who started to eat before this ritual could expect a stern reprimand. These shorter verses led naturally into memorizing longer passages, good preparation for our performances. We took this memorization and delivery seriously because a poor performance would bring laughter from other family members and shame to our parents. My favorite themes were associated with the Easter season. We particularly loved stories of the Passion and passages, such as Matthew 28:5–6, recalling the Resurrection, which evoked for many of us the liberation of Blacks from their earthly burdens.

"The angel said to the women, 'Do not be afraid, for I know that you are looking for Jesus, who was crucified. He is not here; he has risen, just as he said. Come and see the place where he lay.'"

Even as a child, I understood that these passages gave hope to all of us who sought signs of change from segregation and discrimination. When churches staged programs and gave us the opportunity to recite stories of deliverance, I understood that these performances were giving sustenance and meaning to many of the farmers attending the services. I was, with others, doing something constructive to lift others and to help us all have faith in a time when we would be free of the unrelenting challenges we endured.

Typical church services were long. Sunday school began at 9:00 in the morning, followed by the 11:00 A.M. service and, on special occasions, a picnic on the grounds finished the day. Sunday school lessons intrigued me and helped me make sense of the many biblical quotations and references that I heard in the Sunday sermon and in daily references outside of church. I enjoyed the hymns that my mother sang; "The Old Rugged Cross" particularly affected me. Black churches in Grapeland favored passages from the Old Testament, such as Moses leading the children of Israel from Egypt and the stories of Cain and Abel or Ruth and Naomi. In the New Testament, we appreciated the life, death, and resurrection of Jesus. Those who taught Sunday school often had difficulty with the Bible text, but they spoke convincingly about chosen themes once they stopped trying to read aloud for the children. Few adults had a full education, so reading was often a struggle even for the most seasoned of the Sunday school teachers.

Following Sunday school, we were allowed to play outside briefly with other children. We raced around the church grounds, giggling incomprehensibly, but when the service began, we were expected to be in our seats, usually next to our mother, who always wore a serious and devout face. She permitted no laughing, talking, sleeping, whining, or fidgeting.

The service began with a ten- to fifteen-minute devotional period, during which deacons started a long and generally mournful call to worship. This was my mother's favorite part of the service because she loved singing hymns. "What a fellowship, what a joy divine, leaning on the everlasting arms" was more upbeat than many of them, which tended to evoke delivery from suffering and want.

> Guide me, O Thou great Jehovah,
> Pilgrim through this barren land;

I am weak, but Thou art mighty;
Hold me with Thy powerful hand;
Bread of heaven, bread of heaven,
Feed me till I want no more,
Feed me till I want no more.

Mama's favorites always had an eerie reference to eternal rest, as if everyone was happily awaiting the moment when they would ascend to heaven.

Jesus, keep me near the Cross,
There a precious fountain,
Free to all—a healing stream—
Flows from Calvary's mountain.
In the cross, in the cross,
Be my glory ever,
Till my raptured soul shall find
Rest beyond the river.

Since latecomers were not encouraged to disturb the devotional, worshippers who had congregated outside the church filed in noisily as the full service went into gear. The small choir marched in proudly, stepping in time to the music, and took their places behind the pulpit. Their entry and the more uplifting songs they brought were a relief and a contrast to what had come before. After the mournful devotional period, I found the loud, active, and unpredictable part of the service more enjoyable. Now I could see everyone's Sunday Best: polished shoes, hair groomed with pomade or lard, and suits and dresses that had been aired out and pressed. Since most congregants could not shop in stores, their dresses were often makeshift creations with crude home stitching, odd-fitting suits that were clearly out of date, and unstylish shoes. They seemed unaware of any awkwardness of dress. Watching the interactions among them as they proudly displayed their church attire was the best entertainment I had as a child in Daly.

Church decorum was very important and well understood by attendees. For example, in order to move about, convention required one to raise an index finger to beg permission to rise before crouching and tiptoeing silently to one's destination while still holding up a finger. Often those tiptoeing did not need to move but simply wanted the congregants to see their Sunday Best. They would choose a moment for maximum visibility, rise with their finger in the air, and walk across the sanctuary showing off their shoes, hair, and dress. Alternatively, "getting happy" during a song or the sermon, they might attract attention by falling into a trance-like state. Some planned carefully their moment in the spotlight and played this role with a practiced flourish. My mother rarely rose from her seat but would weep softly when the spirit touched her.

In awe of all this activity, I would watch with nervous anticipation as the preacher's sermon heated up to the inevitable moment when the spirit would seize members of the congregation, causing them to "get happy" and shout. Nothing compared to the actors in this live drama. Shouting occurs when a worshipper is overwhelmed emotionally by the service and is transformed into a unique state of devotion, which takes many forms depending on the preference of the worshipper. It can be highly physical, involving jumping, marching, flailing, or virtually any manifestation of sorrow or joy one can imagine. Ushers would stand at the ready to assist those who were shouting by fanning them, holding them down to prevent injuries to others caused by their movement, helping them out of the sanctuary, or whatever might be necessary to calm them. Worshippers would continue to listen to the sermon in the midst of the commotion, sometimes avoiding looking at the person who was shouting. I was transfixed by the behavior of these otherwise stern, staid adults. Many seemed to lose control, falling back and stretching out in undignified ways. I remember one otherwise modest elderly woman who always rose from her seat and walked back and forth down the aisle while rubbing her hands against her outer thighs. "Oh, Lawdy! Have mercy, Jesus!" she moaned. The people who "got happy" contrasted greatly with my composed mother.

The sermons at Greater New Hope and other churches we visited in the Grapeland area provided me with my earliest lessons in human behavior. With few opportunities to observe people outside my family, these encounters started me thinking about how different these churchgoers were from Mama and Daddy. It was hard to understand what was motivating their behavior in church and at the picnics. My mother seemed to have extraordinary insight into who was good and who was bad, but I couldn't understand how she acquired this knowledge. I wondered how my wise mother was able to decipher what was true or false, what was good or suspect,

what was to be trusted and believed. Most important, I wondered if I would ever be able, like Mama, to be as observant
or as discerning.

I came to prize such discernment as I grew older and as
I began to rely more on the meaning rather than the mere
fact of what I was observing. I became aware that there was
more to life than what I saw, more to my future than the
limitations of the present, and more to accomplish than
being merely a helpmeet to a man like my father. I slowly
gave myself permission to think about who I was and what I
could be separate from my family. My early experience observing people in Grapeland and contrasting my impressions
of them with that of my mother began a process that encouraged me to focus on the many differences manifested among
human beings. Were the people who got happy in church
actually transported by their faith or were their antics evidence of their desire to be seen and admired? And how
should one judge their desire to be seen and appreciated? If
they were truly moved, why didn't such feelings descend
upon them instead in a quiet way, causing them to reflect
deeply?

Much later and more incrementally, I began to understand better the challenges of their daily lives. If they were
denigrated during the week, why would they not strut on
Sundays? If they felt hopeless, why would they not focus on
the most uplifting stories from sermons and the Bible? I
began to appreciate the cause and effect of suffering people's
lives and how individuals manage to address or compensate
for overwhelming challenges. Thinking back on the contrast
between the behavior of people on Sundays and what they

suffered during the harsh labor of the week, I began to wonder if I would react in a similar fashion, accepting this dichotomy. How could I prevent my life and actions from being shaped forever by the Murray Farm and the poverty, isolation, and limitations it represented?

4

Latexo

BROTHERS GEORGE AND JOE MURRAY BEGAN ACQUIRING land west of Grapeland around 1911. After a nephew, Arch Murray, joined their farming operation, they formed an ambitious separate enterprise on the banks of the Trinity River that grew to 4500 acres. Known as the Murray Farm, it gradually accumulated tenants who worked the corn and cotton crops. A tornado had swept through in 1935, killing fourteen and injuring sixty-five. By the time my father moved us to the Murray Farm, scores of families were residing there and working the land as sharecroppers. George and Joe were frequently seen on the farm and, somehow, my father developed a side job hauling workers to one of the other Murray-owned farms in the Latexo area, south of Grapeland. Reliable and compliant, Daddy won the confidence and support of the Murrays, and his relationship with the owners led to his being asked to live on and work land they owned in Latexo. We relocated there in 1951, when I was six, continuing a pattern of moving every few years that would endure throughout my childhood. The move from remote Daly to Latexo, only seven miles from Grapeland, made an enormous difference in our outlook as a family and in my future as the youngest child. It opened up new possibilities for my life and set me on the path to learning about the world.

Like so many of the small communities along Route 19 with mysterious names like Lovelady and Cut, Latexo was little more than a few stores, a service station, a café, and some scattered farms. Our Latexo house was far superior to our Murray Farm shack. Rather than being surrounded by a large number of houses, it sat atop a hill looking across fields with only one house nearby. Yet, being on busy Route 19 lessened our sense of isolation.

Crockett, the county seat, six miles from Latexo, was a relatively bustling commercial center. As one of the oldest towns in Texas, it had a number of stately historic buildings that bespoke its position as the most important town in Houston County. Grapeland attracted isolated families from outlying communities who, whenever they went into town, lingered to socialize with people they had not seen for some time. Crockett, in contrast, seemed less a place for farming families from the outskirts to congregate and more a place to get things done. While I could only observe the pace and intensity through a car window as we drove through town, I thought how invigorating it must be to live in a town where people were not just doing backbreaking fieldwork but were otherwise productively engaged. I longed for visits to Crockett in the way that many rural youth long for big-city life. It would be wonderful, I thought, to live in a town with large, attractive buildings; commodious, well-maintained houses; and stores stocked with goods and merchandise manufactured in faraway cities.

Stores figured prominently in our yearnings because we rarely had store-bought goods; we grew the food and made the clothing our family needed. What we couldn't make my parents ordered from a catalog. Repurposed twenty-five- to one-hundred-pound cotton sacks that held the flour and grain we had stockpiled between trips to the general store in Grapeland provided the fabric for our home-sewn clothes. Using flour sacks as fabric for clothing was a tradition dating from my grandmother, who used them and "bed ticking" to make her sturdy clothes. Mama, it is fair to say, was not an exceptional seamstress. She had particular difficulty with the fabric at the tops of sleeves; our dresses, though promising when she started them, were ultimately crude concoctions. These features made us look like the essence of country bumpkins, which, in fact, we were.

Though we had moved closer to Crockett, we did not generally shop there. Wilford had purchased a car for us, but transportation remained an issue with only one car for a large family. We continued to order household items and shoes through the Sears catalog and made do whenever possible with reusable substitutes and hand-me-downs. We made our own milk products and condiments from whatever we had at hand. Discarded syrup buckets typically held our lunches, and empty shoeboxes served as containers for gifts. I didn't miss the fancy containers and wrappings but treasured what these modest substitutes contained. My favorites were the empty shoeboxes that held the only Christmas presents we received: fruits, nuts, and candy.

A long path led from Route 19 to our Latexo house. The vantage point created by the slope down to the highway offered a thrilling view of automobiles speeding along the road to destinations that I imagined to be important. One of our favorite pastimes was inventing games based on the makes and models of the passing cars. In truth, there were few different recognizable models in the area at that time, but our limited knowledge of the world and lack of entertainment nevertheless made this recognition game exciting.

My increased yearning to know about the world beyond Grapeland seemed at last possible to satisfy. In reality, we still had to be careful about venturing out to unknown places. Mama and Daddy taught us at a young age that any area we did not know could be dangerous for Blacks. Stops for gasoline, water, and restrooms had to be plotted carefully, with specific intelligence about which places served Blacks. I thought my parents were exaggerating the dangers, but I would eventually learn that they had reason to be cautious. Entering the wrong door, sipping at the wrong fountain, or asking to use an off-limits restroom were well known to offend those whites who believed upholding racial separation to be their sacred duty. And so, even with greater access to other towns, we avoided approaching the line separating Blacks from whites.

Route 19 led from Latexo to Highway 45, the main road between Houston and Dallas. Elbert, Chester, Wilford, and Atherine had all moved to Houston by the time we relocated to Latexo. Even in those days, Highway 45 was heavily traveled. Going along Highway 19, we passed a series of small towns before reaching Huntsville, which was then and is now primarily notable for its prison. Its electric chair, high security, red clay soil, and hilly terrain gave the town an air of ominous pride, but I was always apprehensive passing through that area. Family members rarely stopped in any of the towns along the route, including Huntsville, but transitioned as quickly as possible onto Highway 45 to make their way to and from Houston. Although we rarely traveled to Houston, living on Route 19 made us feel closer to the family there because the roads from Latexo were much better and faster than those from Daly.

Our Latexo house also gave us a sense of having moved up slightly from our Murray Farm status. Its greater privacy, its accessibility, and its reasonably good condition definitely improved upon our Murray Farm house. My sister Nora always said that, of all the tilting hovels on that vast farm, ours stood out for its especially sorry state. It was in Latexo that I started school and, because of the school bus route, I was able to attend daily, unlike my sisters and brothers, who could not do so when we lived in Daly. Returning home from school in Grapeland, I loved to anticipate the moment when our house would come into view. It stood so solidly, mirroring my feelings of security during a time when school had begun to give me a taste of what life could offer. For a family living constantly on the cusp of want, this home gave us greater legitimacy, stability, and freedom.

The layout of the Latexo house was consistent with that of most of the homes we had in my childhood. We entered through a front room that functioned as a parlor by day and a bedroom at night. A large room to the right held two large iron beds for me, the twins, and Nora—two abed. Arnold, Ruben, and Clarence shared a room behind ours and next to the kitchen. A stove with an L-shaped stovepipe in the parlor provided the only heat outside the kitchen. Occasionally, as a special treat, we roasted sweet potatoes in the stove. As they baked, a sweet, sticky juice would seep through the skin and form dark, aromatic, sugary bubbles. The only thing that equaled our excitement about roasting sweet potatoes was ice cream made from snow. Snow was a rare occurrence in East Texas, and my father would take advantage of the snow-fall by gathering snow, mixing it with canned evaporated milk, sugar, and vanilla extract, and turning it into instant ice cream. Given our lack of a refrigerator or freezer—we had only an icebox—the flavored snow was manna to us.

When my mother was not working in the fields, she was in the kitchen. Her food preparation seemed to continue from breakfast to dinner without interruption. In the late summer, she canned fruits and vegetables in a long produc-tion of peeling, shelling, shucking, and blanching. Anything that could be canned was: tomatoes, okra and tomatoes, suc-cotash, chowchow (a pickled cabbage slaw condiment), peas,

corn, and other vegetables. Occasionally, she canned chicken
and sausage. I especially appreciated the peaches, blackber-
ries, and even tomatoes that she turned into delightful and
treasured desserts during the winter months. When Mama
made jams and jellies, the smell of sugar syrup boiled with
grapes, peaches, and other fruits made us giddy with anticipation. I even cherished jelly made from the muscadine
grapes that grew wild although they were so commonplace
that we often tired of eating them from the vines. Yet when
Mama boiled them, strained out the seeds and hulls, and
made jelly and preserves, I thought she was a miracle worker,
taking this commonplace fruit and turning it into a winter
surprise. Watching the growing array of beautiful jars on
the shelves—green, red, yellow, brown, and variegated—was
like going to the county fair and seeing a veritable festival
of plenty. When arranged on shelves, they proved my mother's ingenuity and further attested to our improved station in
life.

When my mother exhausted her supply of canned goods,
necessity and limitation led her to create foods from otherwise bland basics. My favorite was the improbably delicious
butter roll, a confection made of fluffy dough, which she
sprinkled with butter, nutmeg, and sugar, then rolled up, covered in vanilla-flavored milk, and baked.

Our fascination with food derived from a long period in
my family's history when food was scarce. That time stretched
from my father's fatherless childhood early in the century
straight through my childhood—fifty long years of Stubblefield hunger. When all eleven children were at home (Elbert
was married and out of the house by the time I was born),

there was never enough to eat. This state of affairs prompted near-fatal attempts to find food. One of my sisters once tried to eat a raw bird; another ate lye from a can she found in the house. Although we ate indiscriminately all that was available, a hollow feeling lingered in our stomachs. These feelings were especially present after phantom meals.

Mama's delicious biscuits were always available since we always had enough flour, water, baking powder, and lard on hand. Our phantom meals usually consisted of biscuits with syrup (homemade sugar syrup or store-purchased sorghum) with bacon fat drizzled in for flavor. This sometimes served as our school lunch. Mama put the biscuits in the bottom of an empty syrup bucket and poured syrup over them, making eating lunch rather messy. We would have syrup biscuits for breakfast and lunch and, infrequently, for dinner. Another phantom meal was biscuits and flour gravy, made from browning flour in fat and adding water. On better days, beans or peas with a small amount of fatback and cornbread could serve as the one-dish meal for the family. Even with our hunger, we appreciated Mama's ingenuity in the kitchen. By the time we moved to Latexo, the older children were sending money back to Mama and Daddy from Houston and phantom meals were increasingly rare.

The kitchen was the site of the most important household activities in those years: cooking, canning, making butter, ironing, bathing, and preparing our hair for Sunday church. The production of butter, although especially time-consuming, was easy enough for the youngest children. After we milked our cows, we put some of the milk aside on the cupboard to sour. Placing the soured milk in a churn, a tall cylindrical container from which a long stick protruded through an opening in the top, we would repeatedly plunge the stick and the wooden disk at its end into the churn. Churning separated the fat from the soured milk, and as the butterfat rose to the top, an enticing buttery milk appeared. I loved to anticipate the special treat that Mama would make for our help with churning—hot cornbread soaked in buttermilk and sprinkled with sugar. Or she would make tea cakes, large butter cookies, which we would eat with buttermilk. Many years afterward, when more expensive meals were available, family members still favored buttermilk and cornbread.

Mama was also skilled at ironing clothes and, when we moved to Houston, she worked as a maid and took in huge amounts of ironing to supplement our family income. In Latexo, she ironed only for us. She heated the small, compact iron on the stove between intervals of pressing. The heat of the iron would last only long enough for one section of a garment. With a heavy cloth wrapped around the hot handle, my mother pressed the iron into the clothes, moving it dexterously around sleeves, buttons, and folds.

With the same deftness, she removed kinks from our hair with a combing iron that she heated on the stove. On Saturday nights, the kitchen became a private bath, spa, and beauty shop. She knew how to heat the comb to a temperature that would eliminate the kinks but not burn our hair. She applied Vaseline, pomade, or bacon fat on our hair to facilitate the smooth movement of the comb; then she would pull the comb through the hair, making it straight. Occasionally, the overheated comb would burn, and seared chunks of our hair would fall away. Disguising these damaged patches was difficult, so Mama took great care to test the comb on a piece of fabric before pulling it through our hair. If it burned the fabric, it was set aside to cool before pressing. During the week, Mama and the youngest girls wore plaits or braids, hairstyles that did not require straightening, but for special occasions and church, the youngest girls' hair was hot-combed slightly to make it manageable for arranging in pig-tails or curls. Often the task of straightening or combing my hair was assigned to my older sisters and, resentful, they took little care to avoid inflicting pain while getting rid of my tangles.

My grandmother had worn a headdress and plain clothes, and Mama seemed to follow Mamemma's philosophy that to concern oneself with physical appearance was to be excessively vain and ungodly. Her natural abstemiousness must have pleased my father, since he insisted that she not wear lipstick and makeup. Mama prepared her hair with minimal fuss, most often opting for pinning plaits hard against her skull. Taking no care with her appearance beyond what was necessary to be clean and neat, she wore dresses that were often shapeless, faded, and frayed. When she deigned to straighten and curl her own hair, she used crude paper curlers made from brown paper bags. Tearing the brown paper into small segments, she would fold pieces tightly into three-inch strips and then roll strands of her hair around each section, tying the ends securely. The result, eight hours later, was a head of tight curls that, when combed, dangled stiffly. One couldn't say that this produced a fashionable hairstyle, but it did produce hardy curls.

On Saturdays, we heated great quantities of hot water on

the kitchen stove for a succession of baths before church the next morning. A bath was an important weekend affair, a rare treat that we couldn't help but regard excitedly as a moment of renewal. My father was the only one in the house who got regular access to soap and water in great quantities. The rest of us, including Mama, had to be content with small amounts of each to maintain adequate hygiene. Water was very hard to come by, even in Latexo. It had to be carried in buckets from the well to the house. For ordinary drinking, a bucket was kept at the ready with a dipper inside. A long handle with a cup at the end, the dipper was the common drinking vessel for the family and was shared with anyone who visited. A cool drink of water is very satisfying on a farm, especially during hard labor and intense heat; but, for my mother, a drink of water was more than satisfaction of her thirst. She loved water—the taste of it, the feel of it, even the smell of it as it came from the well deep underground. The doctor had ordered her to drink copious amounts of water because of kidney problems she developed after her pregnancies, but she accepted this requirement gladly because, she said, "What could be better than a drink of water?"

With large quantities of water so difficult to draw from the well and carry inside, it was impossible for all of us to have daily baths. During the week, as we returned from our barefoot work and play in the fields, we washed our feet before going to bed. Even with this ritual, the ubiquitous sand crept into bed with us and inevitably made its way to our hair. In the morning, we could only wash our hands and face and wet-towel ourselves clean, but on the weekend, if we were lucky, we could finally have a real bath with hot water. In the summer, a large tub filled to the brim with water was left to heat in the sun. With temperatures hovering around 100 degrees, this method was efficient and inexpensive, to say the least.

We washed with a harsh lye soap made by my mother through a process that was, I suspect, used by her mother before her. She organized soap making around a huge black iron cauldron in the yard that was used to heat water for a variety of purposes. With a long wooden stick, she stirred lye and lard together until it congealed. When it cooled, she cut it into bars. This soap was used in personal bathing, dish-washing, and cleaning. On laundry day, it was used to wash heavily soiled clothes in the same cauldron. The wash water was stirred to agitate the soiled clothes, and stained sections of clothes were rubbed on a washboard. She repeated this sequence many times until the wash was clean and ready for rinsing, blueing (to freshen the appearance of whites), and hanging on the line. I loved the fragrance of clean laundry dried in the sun. That sunny, fresh smell was newness itself. So was the entire process of bathing, washing my hair, and putting on clean clothes.

In Houston we had, for the first time, a hot-water heater, water from the tap, a dedicated bathroom, and an infinite supply of water without having to draw it, tote it, and boil it. I recognized years later that chores I had regarded as fascinating and enjoyable to watch must have been a great burden to my mother. A hot-water heater, indoor plumbing, store-bought soap, groceries, an electric iron, and a washing machine would have made a real difference in her life. Nevertheless, though harsh and demanding, that work seemed to bring out the best in Mama. She did everything with concentrated good cheer, holding us in check as she worked.

These family rituals radiating from my mother's organization of the household had always taken place, but I became more aware of them when we moved to Latexo. Watching Mama perform these tasks so cheerfully filled me with satisfaction. I studied her as she went about her work, watching for signs that the tears I had seen on the Murray Farm might reappear. Hearing her sing as she worked was reassuring even though the spirituals most often had a doleful undertone. If there was no sign of tears, Wilford and the other boys must be okay, I thought.

In Latexo, I developed a friendship with a white girl my age who lived next door, the first friend I had outside my family and the only white friend I had until I was in college. This friend was so memorable in my early life that I have often been disappointed not to remember her family's name. In my memory, I call her Laura to make it more real to me that she actually existed and that we were close friends.

Her family, sharecroppers who were every bit as poor as we, remarkably, were friendly to us and allowed their children to play with us without restrictions or even oversight. I was unaware of the extent of taboos against Blacks and whites socializing. When not in school, Laura and I played together with no concern for race. We were together for whole days on end, running through the fields, inventing our fun, playing tricks on the animals, and having the run of both families' houses. Our play would start early in the day, often before the rest of the household was stirring. One day she and I were racing through her house and we came upon her married sister and her husband having sex. They paused momentarily to look at us as we ran through their room and then good-naturedly resumed their lovemaking. My friend laughed and kept running. I suspected that if I told Mama what we had seen, she would ban me from returning to my friend's house.

I knew this family only during the little more than a year that we lived in Latexo. Yet the happy memories of this girl helped me to avoid falling prey to the bigotry I later saw among Blacks and whites. I had learned from experience that knowledge of a people is best constructed person by person. When it was time to move away from Latexo, I was saddened to leave this wonderful place and my neighbor. In Houston, I found Black-white proximity, acceptance, and friendship so rare that I did not have another white friend for twelve years.

By far my most important experience of that Latexo year was starting school at W. R. Banks School in Grapeland. That experience began a process of definition and discovery that was to shape not just that period but my entire life. Before I went to school, my days in Daly had been defined entirely by my family's constant presence. Going to Latexo and school in Grapeland introduced me to children my age and opened a door to learning that overwhelmed and delighted me from the very outset. That initial experience with formal learning was to have a lasting impact on my life and, ultimately, on my career.

It is rare to recall the first time that one walks into a classroom, but if one gets struck by lightning the memory and the sensations remain. When I saw the bright, inviting, and well-organized space of my first classroom, it was heavenly to me. When my teacher directed me to a desk that would be mine, I was overwhelmed to think I finally had my own space. Six years of crowding next to my twin sisters with never a space to myself, six years of being the least important person in my house, six years without common learning tools had led me to this glorious day when I mattered enough to have a dedicated personal space. That wasn't all. The woman welcoming me to that classroom seemed heaven sent: she called me "baby," spoke in a reassuring tone, and possessed a voice that made everything and everyone seem important, even me. At my desk were learning materials that I had never had before: writing utensils, paper, and books. I don't recall ever seeing nonreligious books in my home on the Murray Farm, certainly none describing happy animals and children.

I also met a friend whom we called Baby Brother, a first grader like me and the son of the principal. No one had greater respect in our small community than ministers and educators. Everett Eanes was the only Black principal in Grapeland and was therefore someone to be reckoned with. Many schoolchildren feared him. Some thought him to be contemptuous of the poor children who were bused to the school from the outlying farms. By daring to discipline some of my older sisters and brothers, Mr. Eanes had become a declared enemy combatant to my sister Atherine, who was deeply sensitive to any mistreatment of her siblings. So, when my classmate Baby Brother and I took a liking to each other, our relationship became a source of immense interest and humor in the family.

People in Grapeland had a way of embellishing ordinary events and emotions to the point of absurdity. Loud, prolonged, gut-wrenching laughter was one of the few sports to which Blacks could subscribe in the face of daily toil and ignominy, and many applied themselves to it with the intensity of Olympians vying for a medal. The budding relationship between two six-year-olds—one a country bumpkin and the other from a prestigious and well-off family—became a rich source of ridicule and laughter for many years.

We were, it is true, from very different backgrounds. In the forties and fifties consciousness of Black Grapeland, being fair with straight hair was equal to being favored by the gods, and the Eanes family were fair-skinned. I, on the other hand, had a dark face and kinky hair, and my home-stitched clothing reflected the impoverishment of sharecroppers. The improbability of this ugly duckling having a crush on Baby Brother was a delight, its ludicrousness somehow deeply satisfying. In spite of the ridicule, my affection for this boy started a fantasy that was to endure for many years. Baby Brother never spoke of his fondness for me; most of the imagined connection between us was my doing. My fascination with him derived from the fact that he deigned to become my friend, thus elevating my status. Being thrown among people outside of the Murray Farm, I sought some understanding of who I was in relation to the rest of the world. My teacher and Baby Brother helped me to see that I was a person in my own right, not just Ike's baby girl.

When I learned that we would be moving away to Houston, I consoled myself with the thought that Baby Brother would grow up and find me. For years, I anxiously awaited his arrival, but I never saw him again.

5

Miss Ida Mae

WHILE OUR FAMILY LIVED ON THE MURRAY FARM, most of my older siblings could attend school only when no work was required on the farm. That fate would have befallen me as well if we had remained there. School absenteeism, a commonplace among farm families in that era, left large gaps in children's preparation, hobbling their educational progress until they could escape the demand for child labor. Often they had to overcome that deprivation in adult life by seeking high school equivalency certification. My parents had little concern about children missing school because, in our busy household, hard labor was valued above all competing activities. Reading, reflection, or any type of mind work was superfluous and irresponsible by comparison. Sedentary tasks, deemed suspect, often elicited complaints of laziness or good-for-nothingness. Even after the sun set and no fieldwork occurred, other activities weren't allowed because we could not squander the kerosene in the lamps.

In the fall of 1951, our move to Latexo enabled me to take a school bus every day to W. R. Banks School in Grapeland. Rapidly and with welcome intensity, my world opened up. At the age of six, I was introduced to the powerful world of learning by a dedicated, gifted teacher—Miss Ida Mae Henderson. Although I had had no introduction to formal learning, I recall no apprehension when I started school. I walked into my first classroom with thick, unstraightened plaits; large, bulging eyes; a homemade, ill-fitting dress; and the odor of the bacon fat my mother had smeared on my legs to treat my ashy skin. Although I must have been a sight, instead of making me feel homely, different, and unwelcome, Miss Ida Mae made me think that I was the princess of W. R. Banks—equal to or better than any other child in her class.

Accustomed to my family calling me "you ole big-eyed girl!" I found it remarkable that this woman greeted me with "Hello, precious!" or "Good morning, baby!" By telling me I was valued and speaking to me in this way, she invited me into a world of mystery and magic. What would I discover in such a place? Perhaps the key to the realm that I had long imagined, one varied and interesting, where I would be equal to others.

A buxom woman of thirty-four, Miss Ida Mae was unremarkable in personal appearance. Her glasses lent her an air of seriousness in my eyes because I had not known many who could afford eyewear. Comparatively well-off, educated Black women of a similar age often created a fashionable identity for themselves. After all, only a handful of Blacks in Grapeland had the distinction of being college educated. But utility was Miss Ida Mae's guiding principle in all matters. Wearing clothes that were clean, pressed, and presentable; keeping her hair sensibly straightened and styled; and wearing ordinary glasses, she more than made up for the plainness of her appearance. Her focus was on the children and the magic she created for them in her classroom.

The classroom was itself a place of brilliant light unlike any our homes afforded. Every desk and chair was in order, and all educational materials had their proper place. In my eyes, the order of the room suggested the significance of its activities. Most of all, unlike the sounds of work in the fields, the sounds that emanated from Miss Ida Mae's palace were cheerful, even in the midst of intense activity. It was in Miss Ida Mae's classroom that I first felt my personal importance. It was there that I experienced for the first time ownership of a space and utensils designated for my use alone. A desk and chair, books, paper, and pencils may seem little to many. Yet, for me, coming from a people-crowded but sparsely furnished home, where it wasn't even possible for everyone to be seated at the same time, having a place of my own was miraculous. I began to appreciate that the use and development of my mind might be as important as the physical labor my parents more often praised. That discovery would have a profound effect on my life.

Everything seemed possible with Miss Ida Mae. She could do all the things that I wished Mama had time to do: answer my incessant questions about x and y, give me stimulating work, be patient with me, and teach me how to do many things. Her voice was full of light—ever cheerful and controlled. Her graceful gestures and manner of speaking seemed calculated to capture the energy and deepest meaning of whatever she sought to convey. When she was surprised or delighted, her voice soared; when she was calming a disappointed child, her voice deepened to a reassuring hush. Most of all, her enthusiasm for her work and for the individual students seemed genuine.

When she turned her attention to me, I felt that Miss Ida Mae saw me as a great discovery. Approaching me with a smile, she would bend over my work and express admiration for how well I had done. Everything I did in completing an assignment seemed to prompt extravagant praise. I looked forward to her evaluations of my progress and pressed myself to do my work thoroughly. I even tried to imitate the precision and musicality of her voice; the mumblings of farm culture began to fade from my speech even at that young age. I could not understand how such a magnificent person could heap praise on me, an ugly country girl!

Perhaps Miss Ida Mae's praise was so important to me because it was the first that I recall receiving as a child. Her words made me feel like a unique person rather than an appendage to my large family. I don't recall the specific tasks she assigned, but when she needed a child to do something, she often called on me. Her invitations to me to perform tasks like moving small objects and reading aloud in front of the class allowed me to imagine that sharecropping limitations would not forever define me. The more excitement she expressed about whatever I was doing, the harder I tried and the more I wanted to achieve.

Miss Ida Mae knew just what to do for the country children who came to her room. With the exception of Baby Brother, I made no friends among the children in my class. They were an obedient and calm group, absorbing Miss Ida Mae's urgings without noticeable reactions. Didn't they understand how privileged they were to be in her presence? Without a hint of ridicule, she insisted that we could all do the reading and math she placed before us. What an empowering way to introduce children to learning. In my very first encounter with formal education, Miss Ida Mae's enthusiasm convinced me that learning was supremely important, thoroughly enjoyable, and immensely expansive.

Until that year, everybody I knew was an uneducated farmer or laborer who spoke or read with difficulty. To be in the presence of a person who spoke so well was a revelation. I wanted to seize control of these words and make them work for me. I was accustomed to the Black dialect of my family and peers, in which words were truncated, elided, mispronounced. Miss Ida Mae's enunciation made words seem important. It was not "Grapelin" but "Grapeland"; not "chilren" but "children"; not "Rujean" but "Ruth Jean." With her help, I began to speak with deliberate attention to pronouncing final consonants and all the syllables of words. Fascinated with the precision afforded by mysterious multisyllabic words, I began memorizing some that Miss Ida Mae used. I collected words as some children my age collected dolls, stamps, or baseball cards; this pursuit was not merely empowering, it was as if I was inheriting a fortune.

Shortly after I became president of Smith College, I visited Grapeland. To the great surprise of my siblings, one of the prominent white churches there had invited me to speak at a special program held in my honor. Whatever honors I had received up to that time, this invitation was a great triumph to my siblings because when we lived in Grapeland, this very church, and so many others like it across the country, had forbidden Blacks to attend. Miss Ida Mae, then well into her eighties, came to hear my speech and attend the reception afterward. "I'm so happy to see my baby!" she sang out as if I were still a six-year-old. Tearfully embracing her, I was overwhelmed to see this woman who had set me on the path to a career in education. She had introduced me to the simple premise that the life and exercise of the mind bestow enormous power and promise. She provided a beacon that guided me toward achievement through education.

Seeing her after so many years as a student, professor, and administrator, I could understand better why she had such an impact on my life. She was the incarnation of all that it means to be a teacher, a mentor, a guide. Ever hopeful about what human beings can achieve through learning, she was still inspiring young people even though she had retired. Beyond her sweet greeting, she did not say much to me that day. But it struck me more than ever how much her attitude and commitment to her students had influenced my views about education and my attitude toward my own students. I had wanted her to attend my inauguration at Smith, but she was not able to travel. A September 27, 1995, article in *The New York Times* about my appointment at Smith College mentioned that she could not attend but that I had cited her as a teacher who was supremely important in my development. I hoped that she had been pleased with that article.

After seeing her again, I returned to Smith determined to be a light to my students not just while they were at Smith but for the rest of their lives.

I had come from a family in which girls were implicitly expected to be less important, allowing the boys to receive most of the attention. Mama, an old-fashioned wife, taking orders from Daddy and never daring to have any independent ambition outside of the kitchen, was the antithesis of Miss Ida Mae. This educator made me aware that there were women who had jobs, responsibilities, and professions. I must have recognized in Miss Ida Mae a spirit that not only made ambition possible but opened up the world beyond my clan, my community, and my race, and encouraged me to take a more generous stance toward the world.

Racism had reduced my father to a shadow of the man he could have been, and he turned the demeaning arrogance that had victimized him on my mother, making her subservient to him in every way. With Miss Ida Mae, for the first time I saw the kind of independence of spirit that made life free, happy, and meaningful. If learning could lead to such a result, I wanted it to be a part of my life forever.

PART TWO

Fifth Ward

6

Bloody Fifth

I N THE SUMMER OF 1952, WE PILED OUR FEW BELONGINGS
into my brother-in-law's pickup truck and moved 111
miles south to Houston. Latexo had been a happy place
for me, a place of starting school, finding friendship outside
my family, and beginning to discover what I wanted for my
future. Mentors like Miss Ida Mae—in school, church, and
the community—introduced me to an idea of how different
life could be for Blacks, even with the limitations of enforced
segregation. Moving to Houston disrupted for a time my growing comfort with these new experiences and people. I had
never visited my older siblings in the city and felt anxious
about this faraway place.

I imagine that my fun-loving, gregarious father looked
forward to the move to a large city, but my mother would
have been apprehensive, filled with concerns about how the

move would affect her youngest children. In spite of the harsh working conditions, meager pay, trenchant segregation, and minimal services afforded the Black community in the Grapeland area, we managed to have a life that, by virtue of our ignorance of the severity of its deprivation and the company of so many Blacks who shared our state, was satisfying on many levels. Our extended family in Grapeland added to our comfort, for few things tamed our inclination to be anxious better than the presence of scores of relatives nearby. Now we would have to start over without the secure embrace of the Stubblefield, Campbell, and Johnson clans. The fact that the help and guidance of my brothers and sister already in the Houston area awaited us was my only comfort.

In 1952, Houston was already a brash, ambitious city, aspiring to be the center of commerce for the Southwest. With its appetite for growth and prosperity, the Texas identity, already much mythologized, extended across all segments of the state's population, including Blacks and Hispanics. Blacks, too, sported cowboy boots and ten-gallon hats, listened to country music, and spoke Black dialect with a noticeable country twang. The meal of choice was Texas bar-b-que with potato salad and beans, and there never seemed to be quite enough of it in spite of every Black father aspiring to master the art of smoking the meats to tender perfection.

Despite a few big-city refinements brought by a growing array of cultural institutions, Houston proudly cultivated stereotypical Texas roughness and indifference to northern ways. However, Black Houstonians, even those proudly steeped in the cowboy tradition, accepted that their brand of Texas swagger was still tempered by the constraints of segregation and discrimination. Their lives remained separate and unequal.

Arriving in Fifth Ward from the fields of Houston County, we expected little. One of six wards, the area just two miles from downtown Houston had been settled by freedmen following the Civil War. The community bounded by Lyons Avenue, Liberty Road, Lockwood Drive, and Jensen Drive was by 1952 a busy settlement of modest wooden houses arrayed helter-skelter on lots of varying sizes. It was difficult to apprehend an organizing principle in the area. Bounded by those four main arteries, the residents had developed food stores, churches, funeral homes, juke joints, and other essential services wherever space could be found. Two elementary schools, a junior high school, and a high school offered enrollment to the neighborhood's children, who could, for the most part, walk to one of these institutions. In segregated Houston, all Fifth Ward residents were Black, making the area feel like a much larger version of the Murray Farm in Grapeland. There was little governmental effort to afford residents the necessities that other communities took for granted. Health care had been nonexistent until five years earlier, when private donors and the Missionary Sisters of the Immaculate Conception decided to build a hospital to serve the area. Saint Elizabeth's Hospital stood handsomely on Lyons Avenue, joining E. O. Smith Junior High School as one of the two most distinguished looking buildings in the entire ward.

As sharecroppers and farmers migrated to Fifth Ward in the forties and fifties, the area began to earn a reputation for the more outrageous misdeeds of some of its denizens. Many of the new arrivals were so poor that they had to live communally. Dotting the erratic, unzoned grid of this area were mostly small shotgun-type houses with little appeal beyond the shelter they afforded. Combined with the shabbiness of some houses and the open ditches that ran along the streets, the neighborhood had a look of neglect that I noticed even as a six-year-old. It was fitting, then, that the Southern Pacific Railroad would build a large train yard in the area, completing the sense that "anything goes" in Fifth Ward.

My oldest brother and sister, Elbert and Atherine, having married the Hicks twins, Erma Mae and Herman, had initially purchased a house together to facilitate their move to Houston. They lived in that home until they could build separate houses on the lot. After they settled in these new homes, the original property was available for a succession of relatives transitioning to the larger city.

The house we moved into sat on a lot with residences housing family members who had moved to Houston earlier. It was common to jostle more than one house on a lot with little space between them, and that was the circumstance of 4513½ Lee Street. Elbert and his family lived in a five-room house at 4513 Lee Street; my brothers Wilford, Albert, Ruben, and Clarence lived in a rooming house next door; and my parents and us four remaining girls moved into Atherine's former house, in the rear of Elbert's house. Elbert's brother-in-law, Floyd Hicks (another of Erma Mae's brothers) lived on the other side of the rooming house. This compound arrangement was typical of the way many Blacks were able to move to cities.

Our house was typical for the area: it had a parlor, dining area, kitchen, two bedrooms, and one bath. This pragmatic and efficient layout would be replicated in all of our Houston houses: my parents had a bedroom, and all the girls crowded into the other bedroom, two abed. There was no lawn to speak of and merely the hint of a porch that extended the available working and leisure space of the small house. Still this house was evidence of improvement in our family's fortunes: an indoor bathroom, a kitchen with running water and a modern range, and a separate dining area bespoke a luxury I could not previously imagine.

Although we had been allowed to roam the fields in Grapeland and Latexo freely, our parents quickly determined to curtail our freedom once we moved to Houston. We might as well have been confined to a jail cell. The chief reason for their caution may have been the proximity of Lyons Avenue, notorious for its drinking and carousing. However, with the number of residents in our compound, they needn't have worried; many were attentive to our movements. The crowded lot that accommodated Elbert and his family, the Floyd Hicks house, and the rooming house bordered the train yard. For some reason, the noise of the trains did not unsettle me; new to city noises, I relished the hum of activity and the bluster of freight trains. I also drew comfort from the fact that our compound included nineteen family members: Elbert and Erma and their three children; Floyd's family of four; my brothers in the rooming house; and the six of us in our house.

In addition to the three Hicks siblings who lived on this lot, another of Miss Rosa Lee Hicks's children was intertwined with our family. Nora had married my uncle. Aunt

Nora had a bombastic personality. Big and brash with a raspy voice, she always spoke as if she was talking to someone at a great distance. Her imposing figure and protruding stomach matched her forceful spirit. Capable of issuing warnings with such vehemence that children would quickly scurry to follow her directions, she was an almost mythic figure. I found it odd for my brother and sister to have married Hicks twins and for another of their siblings to be my aunt.

Erma Mae was much smaller in stature than her older sister, Nora, and far more refined. Next to my former teacher Miss Ida Mae, Erma Mae had the greatest influence on me when I was in grade school. Although Erma Mae was from Grapeland and had been shaped by the farming culture, her belief that she deserved the best life could offer set her apart from other women I knew. Had the times permitted her a fair chance for a professional career, she would surely have grasped it, so strong was her desire to rise to the middle class and beyond. In that era, few Blacks from Grapeland would have dared to be so explicit about their aspirations, but Erma proudly revealed her goals to all. She spurned laziness or excuses of any kind and insisted that hard work and ambition could overcome the discrimination that seemed to paralyze others. She was especially adamant that her children set high goals, remain in school, and become responsible and independent. Her pride and pragmatic spirit would later have a significant impact on my outlook. I began to follow her exhortations about what girls' lives could be: independent, useful, respected. I especially took to heart her insistence that education could lead to the kind of life I could be proud of. My working hard in school was no doubt a result of her insistence on how important this would be to me. She was right.

At the time we moved to Houston, Mama had seen very little outside of East Texas. Devoted to her one remaining brother and two sisters in Grapeland, she saw them as often as she could, but she took no time to make friends outside the immediate family. In many ways, she was temperamentally suited for a simpler time. Indifferent to modernity, she would have been a contented frontier woman, settling new land isolated from well-populated areas. She was devoted to family and fueled by a few basic principles: be fair, respect others, and live a godly life.

Elbert, on whom she had depended so often for assistance with the other children, was now but a few steps from our home, and his presence must have been reassuring to her. In addition, Wilford was finally back home from the war in Korea and living in the rooming house in front of us. If Elbert was the son on whom Mama relied for good sense and stability, Wilford was the son she treasured for his kind and giving nature. With both boys living on Lee Street, she was comfortable that the move to the city could work. What I did not know was that she had been diagnosed with severe kidney disease and had already lived well beyond the years the doctor had predicted for her. She must have been comforted by the thought that if her health eroded, we younger ones would be safely near her most trusted and mature children.

As I settled into the neighborhood, gradually learning my way around, Elbert and Erma's oldest daughter, my niece Elma, became my daily companion. Born a month before me, she would be in my class at school. Starting second grade at nearby Atherton Elementary School, I knew that her presence would make me feel less out of place, and I was grateful for her company. Being a child of the city, she spoke properly, dressed well, and was liked by those I found so intimidating. I had the air of a country child, in manner, in speech, and, of course, in dress. I was still wearing the cotton sack dresses my mother had made, while Elma and other children in Houston wore enviably mass-produced store-bought clothes. Their clothes were also made of finer fabric in bright colors with complementary trimmings.

I knew that Elma was prettier and more refined than I. This was underscored one day, soon after I arrived in the city, when I heard children's voices at my brother's house and ran over, planning to join in the play. As I approached, I recognized Elma talking about someone with another girl from the neighborhood, and my instinct told me to slow down and listen before revealing my presence. I was taken aback that they were talking about me and my sisters and how ridiculous we looked in our country clothes. Having a sense of how others viewed us made me cling even more to Elma's example as we went off to school together.

Thick, crude plaits protruding in different directions, ill-fitting shoes that gave me a strange waddle, and the homemade dresses that I wore repeatedly made me the object of laughter. I was anxious to learn how to imitate the behavior, appearance, and speech of these children who were making fun of us. Elma offered the best example of what I should strive to become. Not only did she have her parents' good looks and the poise one would expect of Erma Hicks's oldest daughter but, even at age seven, she had an aura of confidence. She was expected to succeed in anything she tried. I envied everything about her. Being aunt and niece in the same class made us a noticeable duo. Teachers had a tendency to compare us, stoking our competition but pointing out that Elma was the star.

Atherton Elementary School was just four blocks from our compound. I was excited to attend a school that did not require an extended school bus ride. Though only an elementary school, it was as big as the entire kindergarten through high school building of W. R. Banks School for Colored Students in Grapeland. It was also newer, fancier, and more amply supplied, and had many more activities. I was especially impressed with the festive school assemblies on special occasions, the thoughtful promotion of school spirit, and the extensive involvement of parents. Thanks to Miss Ida Mae, I arrived in Houston at second-grade level and was easily able to do the work. Going to school no longer aroused in me the excitement it had in Grapeland, but, determined to keep up with Elma, I applied myself to succeed in this new setting.

Across from Atherton Elementary on Solo Street was the Julia C. Hester House, founded in 1943 to provide character-building, athletic, and intellectual enrichment programs for Black youth in the Fifth Ward. Over time Hester House became a prominent part of my life, opening doors to opportunities that I could not have known otherwise. A modest one-level wooden structure that could barely contain the activity when many children were present, Hester House allowed us the chance to meet others our age through activities such as sports and dances. What I most loved, however, was its small library, where I could borrow books. I imagined this as my own library, where I could have access to books as often as I wished. The period, reading level, or genre did not matter; access to the wealth of words in books such as *Little Women* and *Jane Eyre* was almost as important as the stories and characters they offered. I was still on a mission to acquire as many words and meanings as possible. The festooned curtains and furnishings of the red-room described by Jane Eyre set my heart aflutter. If I could describe things with a similar precision, I could express confidently who I was and who I sought to be. I saw a way forward.

Diagonally across Lee Street from our house was a bar called the Dew Drop Inn. On weekends we could hear the noise from its drunken customers. Couples often launched into loud quarrels that I could hear late into the night. My brothers paid a visit to the Dew Drop from time to time—without Mama's knowledge. The bar entered the annals of Houston crime one dark day when Tommy Head, whose family owned the Dew Drop, killed several members of his estranged wife's family. But in general, by day, my area of Fifth Ward was an ordinary neighborhood where residents went to work in the morning and returned at night to quiet lives behind their unlocked doors.

My father found a job as a custodian at Bama, a maker of jellies and preserves. At the time Bama was a particularly challenging place to work because white workers frequently baited Black workers with racial comments. In Grapeland, even I had noticed Daddy's compliant behavior toward whites. Lacking the surliness that many men adopted in the face of racial discrimination, he seemed to relish playing a subservient role and happily stepped off the sidewalk when a white man or woman passed, saying "Yas-SUH!" and grinning constantly in the presence of whites. These well-practiced strategies contributed to his adapting well to the environment at Bama. He was a popular and permanent fixture there until he retired. Honest, hardworking, and reliable, he had job stability almost immediately, an unusual circumstance for a Black man at the time.

Mama had never learned to drive, so her movements were severely circumscribed. Somehow, that suited her. When she was not working, she spent her days preparing meals and performing household duties that, with access to certain conveniences, were far less burdensome than in East Texas. No more boiling clothes in the yard, making lye soap, or curing meat in the smokehouse. Now she had to purchase everything. Peddlers traveled up and down the street selling fruits and vegetables out of their trucks and wagons. Mama would buy just enough potatoes, tomatoes, or other produce for a day. Additional essentials—insurance, shoes, knives, spices, soaps—came via traveling salesmen. Occasionally, Mama would send us to Schweikardt Street to the Chinese grocer, but most of the time my father did the grocery shopping.

My father insisted on holding on to all the income in the house. When my sisters and brothers got jobs, they had to give him all their earnings. Daddy believed that children should become responsible for themselves as soon as possible, even if it meant dropping out of school. With an eighth-grade education, he had only the most rudimentary sense of where education could lead, and he identified it as a privilege we could ill afford. Like others traumatized by the depression, he was parsimonious in the extreme. To petition him for money was a terrifying and futile act. In the city school system, students' families were asked to provide many things: supplies, gym uniforms and sneakers, clothes for special events, and so on. We learned quickly that we would have to tell our teachers we could not get many of these things. When my sister Nora, only sixteen, went to work cleaning houses to earn money to pay for school needs, my father exacted a major part of her earnings. So she steadily increased her hours to net more income. Eventually, after the tenth grade, she asked if she could stop school to work full time. My parents agreed. Had it not been for legally enforced school attendance, most of the younger siblings would not have finished school. The lax enforcement in Grapeland meant that almost all of the older children had stopped school to work. Once we moved to Houston, all the youngest of us except Nora were able to finish high school without feeling pressure to drop out. But my father would not help us with school expenses.

Mama, however, was more attentive to our needs. She had no more education than Daddy, but she understood how embarrassing and painful it was for us to go to gym class and not be able to participate because we did not have a proper uniform. Intuitive and smart, she did the only thing she could to make sure we had as much as possible: she went to work as a maid.

Yet in spite of all that she was doing for us, the more I saw of city life, the more I began to feel that my mother's old-fashioned standards and lack of style stymied our enjoyment of Houston. For me, her plainness was a growing source of

irritation and embarrassment. Perhaps I transferred onto her
the embarrassment I felt about being a misfit because of my
clothes, speech, and manners, but she was definitely a contrast to the mothers of my schoolmates, who dressed stylishly
and wore makeup and modern hairdos. Mama did not seem
to understand or care that the city required a new approach.
My sister-in-law Erma Mae, however, was different.

Erma Mae was the epitome of what the modern woman
could be: attractive, fun-loving, forceful, direct, independent
of mind, and ambitious. Erma said that women could do
their own thinking. Education was the key, and her girls were
going to be educated so that they could be successful in their
own right. As devoted as Erma was to my brother Elbert, she
did not believe marriage required blind subservience. She
was rearing Elma, Lawanna, and Beverly to be self-assured
girls who set high expectations for themselves. I wanted to
emulate Erma.

I don't know if Mama was aware that I was discrediting
all that she stood for. Perhaps I showed it in the flip answers
I learned to give, in the airs I adopted in imitation of others,
or in the way that I idolized Elma and Erma Mae. I began to
develop a manner of speaking that was affected and stilted,
reminiscent of actresses we saw in the movies. I later modeled my speech after that of Tallulah Bankhead, a prominent
actress at the time. I was openly dismissive of practices that
evoked country living. It certainly did not occur to me until
years later that Mama would have had more appealing clothing and a more polished appearance if she had not put our
needs ahead of hers.

I continued to do well at Atherton Elementary School,

making perfect grades and following rules for student behavior and good work habits. As a result of the continuous positive feedback I was receiving, my confidence grew. At first I feigned confidence, but eventually my comfort with who I was became real. I met friends, broadened my experiences, and began to realize the potential to achieve beyond what my parents imagined for me. Watching Elbert and Erma every day, hearing how they conceived of the future, made me think that their vision might be within reach. Too young and inexperienced to understand how to piece it all together, I nevertheless absorbed Erma's insistence that the future of girls would be different if we would only take charge of it.

A couple of years after we had become accustomed to our first Houston neighborhood, Daddy decided to move us to another implausibly crowded lot, on Sam Wilson Street, just east of Lockwood. There, the landlord, an aspiring real estate magnate named Mr. Woodrow, had constructed or moved to the site a number of shabby houses for which he exacted unreasonable rents. My new neighborhood was like the Lee Street area without the railroad yard or the Dew Drop Inn—rows and rows of poorly kept wooden houses that families rented from landlords unable to maintain them properly. Aunt Aggie, the youngest of Mama's sisters, moved into a house in the rear of ours. Though just a few blocks from Lee Street, this home was much farther from Atherton School, where I remained enrolled through the fifth grade. On Sam Wilson Street, we created a new compound with a different extended family. Mama's warnings about outsiders remained in force, and Aunt Aggie's children substituted for Elma and her sisters.

The Mount Lebanon Baptist Church, located on Lockwood two blocks from our new house, had welcomed Daddy as an assistant minister. My discerning mother liked the pastor there, Reverend Emmitt Thompson, a tall, handsome, and well-spoken young minister who was well educated and dedicated to keeping children interested in the church. All of the pastors I had known before were older, self-taught, and not interested in young church members. I admired Reverend Thompson not only for his attentiveness but for his youth and appealing way of preaching. The bombastic preachers of Grapeland were all about form, but he delivered intelligent, well-composed, thoughtful messages and was among the most charismatic speakers I had ever heard because he did not instill fear about going to hell but, rather, spoke in moving ways about how we should live up to our values. He seemed so perfect that I hoped I would be as lucky as Mrs. Thompson and find a husband with his temperament, good looks, and style. He was a great contrast to my father.

Some time before, Daddy had been "called" to the ministry. He felt that God had revealed to him his duty to follow and disseminate the word of God. Studying the Bible, he apprenticed with ministers and was eventually ordained. Neither a gifted orator nor a commanding singer, he was somewhat awkward in the pulpit. When my father read from the Bible, his delivery lacked feeling, the words stumbling from his mouth with little effect or meaning. His singing was just as unrefined. He would talk halfway through the hymns and hit the especially important notes in a veritable half-shout, distracting listeners from the fact that he was off-key.

A Black Baptist minister of that era who could not sing

had little prospect for a promising career. However, being called to the ministry was a venerated tradition in the Black Baptist church, so people tolerated these limitations. Reverend Thompson invited Daddy to serve in a quasi-official capacity as an assistant minister, which meant he was able to be seated in the pulpit every Sunday. I mentioned to my mother that it was strange to see Daddy in the pulpit, occasionally reading the scripture, and cheering on Reverend Thompson when he preached, given what we saw of him at home, ordering her around and inflicting punishment on his children. She chastised me for speaking ill of him and told me that I was never to do so to others. Still, I began secretly to question the legitimacy of my father's calling. How could a man of God fall so short in his personal life and still have the audacity to teach others how to be godly?

Harrowingly dull, Daddy's sermons ambitiously tried to imitate the cadence and pattern of great preachers, but he would lapse into a droning voice halfway through. Try as he might, he could not achieve the magnificent crescendo to which great sermons generally built. Mama would listen appreciatively, though, no doubt thankful that her husband was trying so hard to follow the straight and narrow after a youth of hell-raising. Daddy's sermons made Azella, Ozella, and me quake with suppressed laughter. But if Mama caught us ridiculing Daddy, we were sure to be punished. Yet we persisted in our antics because making fun of him gave us great comfort at the end of a week in which he would have beaten and berated his children as well as ordered my mother around.

In spite of his harsh, mercurial nature, my father could be generous from time to time—a gift without a special occasion, a kind word unanticipated. His raucous laughter was the best gift. He continued to regale us with his fables, although he was still first in line to laugh appreciatively at his own tales. Despite his obsequious "Yas-SUH!" routine for whites, he was a fierce defender when any of his children was attacked or threatened. My sister Nora came home crying one day after a man on the bus accused her of stealing his wallet. The bus driver asked a woman passenger to search Nora. When Daddy heard this, he took his pistol, gathered my brothers, and followed the bus route, overtaking the bus. He ordered the terrified driver to tell him who had falsely accused my sister. This irrational act seems extraordinary for my meek father, but there were many such stories of his confronting men, Black and white, who had offended one of my sisters. Although this reckless behavior worried me, it also periodically tempered my disappointment in and anger toward him for the way he expected subservience from Mama.

By the time I was eleven years old and about to enter the sixth grade, Daddy had moved the family from Sam Wilson Street to Liberty Road. His wanderlust was puzzling since, for the most part, the quality of our houses didn't improve. Liberty Road offered more space for us, however. The large white house had a sweeping veranda along one side, and there was an ice cream shop attached to the front. Just sitting on the grand porch watching people pass on a busy thoroughfare was a whole afternoon's delight. Inside, there was enough room for all of us. Arnold, back from his army service and married to Fronette, moved into a house at the rear of the property. Azella and Ozella, a year ahead of me in school, could walk from our house to nearby E. O. Smith Junior High

School. I had to transfer to a new school, which, for the first time in my life, I would attend without my sisters. Though I was fearful of this change, in the end I found it easy to adjust to the Quitman Avenue Elementary School and, a year later, I started junior high at E. O. Smith.

E. O. Smith Junior High School was a large stucco building on Lyons Avenue that came to have iconic status in the Fifth Ward. It had been the site of Wheatley High School until the student population outgrew its capacity and the high school was moved to a new building on Market Street. In the tradition of other Fifth Ward schools, the teachers of E. O. Smith shaped generations of achievers in the Black community. Segregation drove Black teachers to Black schools, affording students the best minds that the Black community produced during the pre-civil-rights era. Exceptional teachers at E. O. Smith made learning challenging and enjoyable for me, and one of them, Mrs. Modria Caraway, my social studies teacher, had a significant influence on my direction in life.

Mrs. Caraway was very dark, with a broad forehead that was even more exposed because of her thin hair. Her skin was beautiful, and she was scrupulous about makeup that enhanced her looks. One couldn't say that she was a beauty by any means, but her dress, makeup, and hair made us aware that she was a person who was attentive to every aspect of her appearance. She had a droll and entertaining wit that often prompted her to make shocking comments to her classes. There was little temporizing in her approach; her tongue was sharp and her criticism quick and unmoderated. She spoke to us about sex, about associating with the wrong

types of friends, and about the importance of making something of our lives. Insisting that our success would rest on
whether we understood the lessons of history, she forced us
to memorize important dates and events. She would regularly
remind us, "You cheerin had better listen to me and do your
work, or you're going to be just as ignorant as those niggas
you see standing around on Lyons Avenue." We would laugh
delightedly at her outrageous, though racist, comments.

Mrs. Caraway took a special interest in me and Elma, my
niece, who was again in my class. She thought Elma was
perfect, and she said so with some frequency, always adding
parenthetically that I was smart, too, if not as smart as Elma.
The two of us assisted her with special classroom tasks, such
as collecting assignments, cleaning the room, and writing on
the blackboard. During the summers, she invited me to her
home. Her husband owned a dry-cleaning shop in Third
Ward, and her sister, Mrs. Dorothy Peters, also became my
mentor and friend. Mrs. Caraway's exceptional interest in
students and their lives made her stand out among my teachers. She spoke to us of life, of the risks we faced as Blacks, of
the problem of teen pregnancy, of the racial issues we would
face, and of the hopeful possibilities that might exist for us.
Although her outspoken humor invariably prompted laughter
from her classes, she was exceedingly serious about serious
matters. Once I got past her odd speech and mannerisms, I
began to learn much about the subject she taught and benefited from her personal commitment to her students.

Counselors like Mrs. Punch, the principal, and teachers
like Mrs. Caraway at E. O. Smith helped me to understand
that, by working beyond the curriculum, which they freely

admitted was tailored to students of less ability and interest, I could prepare myself for a much more challenging academic experience. Although they did not offer algebra, one teacher, Mrs. Washington, took it upon herself to introduce me to the subject. Indeed, every teacher sought out books for me and designed extra assignments, pushing me to the next level even when it meant that they had to spend time outside of class.

Mrs. Caraway alerted me to the need to follow current events and brought in newspapers and magazines to demonstrate that there was much to know beyond what the social studies textbooks covered. I especially enjoyed national news coverage of President Dwight D. Eisenhower since we had an Ike in our family. The contrast between the two evoked many jokes in our household. The continuing fallout from the Supreme Court's *Brown v. Board of Education* decision desegregating public education led to animated discussions in Mrs. Caraway's classroom. Cultural awareness was no less important to her than the approved curriculum for which she was responsible. Though limited in what we could do in segregated Houston, her emphasis on Black activists, cultural figures, and literary works helped us understand what might be possible in a world of broader access.

In junior high, we again had to buy extras. Sorting out how I was to secure the needed items was an ongoing challenge. With considerable dread, I came home one day to tell my mother that I had to have a pair of tennis shoes for gym class. Asking my father was out of the question. It pained me to know what those tennis shoes would cost my mother in toil and sacrifice.

From time to time, when I was not in school, I would accompany Mama to her job to help out in small ways. Observing her at work was enlightening. She went about her work
cleaning other people's houses with the seriousness and pride
I had always seen her apply to her chores at home. She
showed me how to complete the work satisfactorily and insisted that I never "half-do" anything. Whether folding clothes,
sweeping and mopping floors, or making beds, she taught me
how to do chores precisely and correctly. That she was showing me this in another family's house was unsettling. I wanted
Mama to resent having to clean white people's houses, but
she showed no hint of anger or resentment about her work.
Her employers treated her with respect, although I did not
like them calling her "Fannie" and her having to address them
as "Miss Such-and-Such."

As we grew older, Mama's being so strict about our involvement in activities became more and more of a problem.
My junior high classmates were beginning to go to dances and
date, but these were out of the question for me. I was starting
to like particular boys, but I was terrified of what Mama and
Daddy would say if any boys wanted to visit me. I had a crush
on Mickey Leland when I was at Atherton, and I continued to
worship him and his cousin James from afar. Mickey reminded
me somewhat of Baby Brother; both were fair-skinned. He
later went on to great fame as a civil rights fighter and con-
gressman. Despite such attractions, I deflected the overtures
of most boys, focusing instead on my studies and on the activities that I was allowed to participate in.

When I graduated from E. O. Smith Junior High School,
the theme of the ceremony was "The Responsibilities of Our

Generation." Elma delivered the Class Pledge, and I gave a brief speech of thanks from the graduates. I was surprised to learn that I was the highest-ranking student in the class. While I had been aware that I was doing well, I had not realized I was doing better than Elma. I didn't celebrate that fact but took it as a fluke, anticipating that my niece would ultimately achieve more than I. Nevertheless, we were both on our way as Erma Mae wanted.

The words on the front of the graduation program, by Harriet Ware, spoke to the new power we felt:

This day I will be conscious of my heritage!
I am a child of Him who made the sun and stars.

7

Canaan

B Y THE TIME I STARTED AT PHILLIS WHEATLEY HIGH
School in 1960, it was probably the most prominent
school for Blacks in Houston, with an exceptional
record of transforming students from the Fifth Ward into notable achievers. In the midst of Fifth Ward, Wheatley was a
village within a village—an academic and social oasis for the
young people of the area. Coming to grips with the changes
that might occur as a result of the Civil Rights Movement
and an end to racial segregation, residents considered the
possibilities that might lie ahead for Wheatley graduates.
With city buses desegregated and lunch counters being integrated, many had begun to anticipate the further integration
of Blacks into the mainstream. I was not, at the time, significantly attuned to those possibilities. The still low expecta-

tions of my parents and others tempered my thinking about the possibility of equality.

Houston's population had doubled to nearly one million in the eight years since we had moved to the city. There had been numerous legal attempts to desegregate the public schools and, in November 1960, just as I was starting at Wheatley, the Supreme Court rejected a last-ditch appeal from the Houston School Board to defer integration once again. Yet, with all the change expected, in our academic oasis on Lockwood and Market, many of us were too confident about the worth of Wheatley to care about the results of these efforts to gain admission to white establishments. White schools could not, we thought, be better than Wheatley.

In fact, living in Fifth Ward afforded us access to numerous institutions that formed a loosely coordinated network to help us advance. The Black teachers and administrators in the area elementary and junior high schools understood well what we needed to prepare us for high school; insistence on basic language, science, math, and social science knowledge shaped their curricula. Fifth Ward churches and community centers, including Hester House, offered resources for families without the means to provide academic and cultural enrichment to their children. We frequented their programs and often gained poise and confidence from them. With thriving youth programs that encouraged strict morality and behavior, church pageants provided opportunities for artistic and cultural growth. We joined youth choirs and performed in musicals and seasonal plays. For every juke joint and liquor store that drew many people on both weeknights and weekends, there were opportunities to build the skills and know-how of Fifth Ward's children so that they would be ready for full citizenship.

Although our original compound on Lee Street had given us a hopeful outlook on the transition to Houston, by 1960 we saw our living accommodations slide to a sorry state. We rented a house at 4432 Sumpter Street, where we moved to be closer to Wheatley, but it was little more than a hovel. Infested with rats and roaches, it was reminiscent of the conditions on the Murray Farm. Its greatest asset was a small porch across the front. Set off the ground on cinder blocks, the house had five rooms. Without a foyer, we entered the house from the porch through two front doors. The door on the left led to our parents' bedroom and the other door to a small sitting room. That room, where we spent most of our time, was just big enough for a sofa, chair, and television. A dining room adjoined the living room, and behind it was a kitchen. Three rooms made up the other half of the house. At the front next to the living room was Mama and Daddy's bedroom. A small hallway led to the one bathroom and the girls' bedroom. Across the back of the house was an enclosed porch, part of which served as my brother Clarence's room (Ruben had married and was no longer staying with us).

In spite of its state, Mama took care of this house as if it were worth the trouble. She carried out all of her duties with a degree of dedication that I couldn't understand. Her day began at about 4:00 A.M., when my father rose to get ready for work at the jelly factory. She would prepare him a hot breakfast of bacon, eggs, biscuits, and syrup, over which he would linger to slurp his coffee. He was fond of pouring his coffee into the saucer, blowing on it, sipping it loudly, and letting out a satisfied "aaah!" At 4:30, we would be wakened by his bath, which was exceedingly noisy, and then kept awake by his eating and slurping. We were convinced that he was deliberately trying to rouse us from our sleep. It was unclear why he couldn't rise quietly and go to work without making Mama get up to fix his breakfast. But once Daddy left, Mama, whom we assumed must be exhausted, would not go back to sleep. Aunt Aggie, who had moved into a house on the next street, would come over to visit. Their chatter further disrupted our sleep, and we couldn't imagine what they had to talk about so early in the morning.

We should have been happy to see Mama relaxing and enjoying her sister's company. If only we had known what awaited us. My mother's health had been tenuous since the birth of Azella and Ozella in 1943. Almost a decade later, when we were preparing to move to Houston, she would have recognized that, given the doctor's dire prognosis of potential kidney failure, her life expectancy was uncertain. My older sisters knew of her condition; we younger ones did not. My ignorance of the decline in her health allowed me to go about my Wheatley years without a care about any looming problems.

My youngest brothers, Ruben and Clarence, had become star players on the Wheatley basketball team and I was proud to enter the high school as their youngest sister. Their achievements at school, however, did not cause them to be more generous to us at home. My brothers were treated with deference and not required to do any work around the house. They always seemed to get preferential treatment. If they entered a room and found us sitting in a chair they wanted, they demanded we move, knowing that any protest of their behavior would be unanswered. Yet, as oppressed as they made us feel at home, when we got to Wheatley, we were happy to be known as their younger sisters. I was to experience the same feeling many decades later when I became president of Clarence's alma mater, Prairie View A&M University. For many at that university I was only Clarence's younger sister and, oddly, after so many accomplishments, I was proud to be known that way.

Ruben, handsome and serious, with deep-set eyes, was popular among his peers. Because of his tough-guy demeanor, few would challenge him, even my father. Though imposing, he was not tall but usually wore an intense, sober expression that made everyone cautious about not heeding everything he requested. Even my father kept his distance from Ruben and would lend him his car from time to time, a gesture that dumbfounded the rest of us. Ruben once had an accident while driving my father's car. We would all have been terrified to confess such a transgression to Daddy, so we pressed Ruben about what he was going to do. He responded calmly, "I'm just going to tell him what happened." He did just that and when Daddy did not scold him for the accident, Ruben seemed to become even more formidable.

Clarence followed Ruben onto the basketball team and, for a brief time, they were on the team together. While we younger sisters revered Ruben, we thought Clarence was just plain weird and maybe "a bit off." He always pretended to play basketball and, as he was doing so, he would talk to himself. We did not notice this while Ruben was still at home because he and Clarence were always together. Both had jobs and moved about on their own without permission from my parents. After Ruben graduated and married and Clarence was the only boy at home, he was consumed by improving his basketball skills. Since we couldn't afford equipment at home, he turned objects at hand—clothes, paper, cans, anything—into basketballs or goals. He spent hours in his room making real and imaginary jump shots, providing sound effects and play-by-play commentary for every move and every score. The ruckus made us think he should be committed to an institution for the mentally unsound, and we insisted to Mama that "something needed to be done about that boy."

Clarence graduated from Wheatley in 1960, the year I started there. His skills had earned him a basketball scholarship at Prairie View and he became the first of us to attend college. At the time, I asked Mama if I might be able to attend college one day. Pausing briefly in her chores, she responded, "If we can get the money . . ." her voice trailing off. I sensed that she did not think it would be possible. That I would return fifty years later as president of the very university that started our family's journey to higher education and the middle class has been a source of great satisfaction to me. I'm certain it would have been the same for Mama.

As the younger sister of basketball stars, I began high school with renewed enthusiasm for school. With the expanded social studies reading that Mrs. Caraway had insisted

I complete, I was more than ready for high-school-level work. With knowledge of history and current events, and having benefited from her civics instruction both in and outside the classroom, I was well informed about a variety of subjects. The Wheatley library, better than any I had had access to before, was a welcome source of books for my ever-expanding reading list. This list was not purposeful; rather, it focused on volume. My intent was to read as many books as possible of every genre as if my future depended on what I could retain from reading the broadest array of information. *Jane Eyre* and *Ivanhoe* were among my favorites, although I appreciated poets like Paul Laurence Dunbar, Langston Hughes, and Edgar Allan Poe just as much. I gravitated most toward literature, wanting to learn specific ways language could open doors to unfamiliar worlds and help me overcome the powerlessness that derived from my family's poverty. I loved the way writers created layers of meaning that enriched one's understanding of human psychology and behavior.

HAVING WORKED DILIGENTLY TO RID myself of the country accent that was typical of those I knew from Grapeland, I didn't want to replace it with the Black urban dialect of Houston. I decided that only the most proper English would help me shed the dust and rags of my Grapeland years. My speaking in a stilted, pretentious manner, sharply enunciating rather than eliding syllables, was shocking to some and resented by others. One of the most serious offenses one could commit was snobbishness, so I was persistently labeled "seditty" and avoided by peers for putting on airs. This shunning was less important to me than my success in creating a new persona. I suppose I thought that elocution was the best means of showing that I was smart and not limited by my family's means or how I looked. Since the moment I discovered that I was being ridiculed for my country air, I determined to work assiduously to prove that I was worthy of respect.

My teachers at Wheatley embraced the notion that they were creating future Black leaders and drilled into us the fact that we could achieve because we were Wheatleyites. Wheatley teachers tended to be well spoken and well dressed, demonstrating to their impoverished students what respectable society would require of them. Mr. Sanders, suave and always nattily dressed, appeared bookish and engaged in delightfully witty repartee. Miss Farnsworth was also stylishly dressed; every detail of her outfits seemed perfectly chosen and fitted for her slim physique. With blond hair and fair skin, she was nevertheless unmistakably Black, but we wondered if she was of mixed race, cast aside by a wealthy white parent. Unfamiliar with any affluent Blacks, we opined that nothing else could explain her expensive wardrobe. Her elegant clothes were to play a surprising role in my life as I prepared to go off to college.

The pride of these teachers in their appearance and in how they conducted themselves reflected their enjoyment of their professional life and made me want to work even harder. That pride was the motif in all that they conveyed to us about who we were as Blacks and what we could become. Phillis Wheatley figured significantly in their urgings. Though her poetry was not taught in any class I took, teachers repeatedly reminded us that she had overcome slavery to become a pub-lished poet in the eighteenth century. Her writing style and subjects, unlike those of James Weldon Johnson and Langston Hughes, did not fit their educational purpose. They thought that the mere facts that she overcame low expectations and became a poet were the most important aspects of her story. In a glass case just inside the turquoise doors to Wheatley on Market Street there was also a display of trophies, photo-graphs, and memorabilia representing the school's illustrious record in sports. These efforts to instill school pride were suc-cessful in lifting our spirits and raising our sights. We could do, and possibly exceed, what others before us had done, they told us.

At Wheatley I began to challenge Mama's strict rules about where I could go and with whom I could associate. She remained mistrustful of the streets of Houston and enforced an as-soon-as-school-is-over-you'd-better-come-straight-home rule. Misfortune could befall girls who lingered, she insisted, and such behavior would make us too available for trouble to snatch us up and carry us off to a life of shame and pain. In Mama's colloquies with my aunts, my sisters and I heard ex-amples of girls who "got in trouble" because their parents were not attentive to the dangers children faced from the fast world on the streets. The worst one could say about a girl at that time was that she was "fast" or "womanish," always pro-nounced "womnish." Mama had no intention of letting us succumb to the bad influences of the big, noisy, dangerous city. When we were not within her sight and reach, a member of our family had to be with us as guard and guide.

How Mama would have known about such dangers was a mystery. In the eight years since our arrival in Houston, I never knew her to attend a civic, social, or cultural event: not a movie, a party at a friend's home, a school program, or, actually, any place other than church, relatives' homes, and the houses she cleaned.

Occasionally, she went to a store, but Daddy steadfastly insisted that the weekly "making groceries" was his important and sole responsibility. Determined to control household spending, he would shop without regard for any individual or family preferences or even a list from Mama. We were prisoners of Daddy's unchanging shopping list. He bought the same food staples from week to week: bacon, eggs, canned biscuits, canned vegetables, dried beans, canned salmon or mackerel, syrup, ground beef, and grain. Mama assuaged our resentment by serving our favorite dishes for breakfast, dinner, and dessert. Transforming the rice Daddy bought in large quantities, she would make us a hot cereal with canned milk, butter, and sugar, and then the same ingredients, plus artificial flavoring and nutmeg, would be fashioned into a delicious baked rice pudding.

In junior high school, I had begun to see how different my social life was from that of other students. I wanted to challenge the restrictions on my movements, which I judged arbitrary when compared to the friendships, freedom of movement, and social engagement that my brothers and others from E. O. Smith seemed to enjoy. Change was difficult under Mama's watchful eye, which surveilled not just what we did but also who our friends were and how their families

behaved. It would not be fair to say that she was a snob, because she had no care for status and generally accepted and
respected people without regard for their social, economic,
or familial circumstances, but she was inflexible when it
came to the Stubblefield tenets of good behavior and character. Once a friend in the sixth grade was visiting me when her
mother came to pick her up at our house on Liberty Road
smelling of liquor. One of the fundamental rules of our house
was "thou shalt not drink liquor," so while Mama was polite
and accommodating to my friend and her mother during their
visit, she pronounced her sentence as soon as the two de-
parted. I was not to see my friend again outside of school and
never to visit her home. Such firm condemnations seemed
even more preposterous and unjust when I started high
school and made friends who enjoyed far fewer restrictions
on what they could do.

Still, once I arrived at Wheatley, I understood the consequences of ignoring Mama's dicta. Those consequences lingered in my mind after an unsuccessful effort to challenge
them two years earlier. Scheming with a friend from junior
high school who invited me to Sunday morning service at his
church, I began planning how I could escape Mama's view
long enough to get to church on Lyons Avenue. Going to a
different church was hardly a bold way to rebel, but it was
the ideal way to point out my mother's hypocrisy and the
thinness of her reasoning. If I could not even go to church
with a friend, her rules were patently senseless, petty, and
arbitrary. This would become clear to Mama, I was sure. Had
such rules been in force for Ruben and Clarence, they never

would have been allowed to spend hours on the basketball court at Hester House and at practice at Wheatley, or to compete in district and state games. Being on the teams gave them a way to fit in, to become familiar with a world that the rest of us barely knew. How was I to find my way to college if Mama didn't allow me to have some freedom?

BACK WHEN WE WALKED TO E. O. Smith every day, I had to travel down notorious Lyons Avenue, the center of nightlife in Fifth Ward. "Lines" Avenue, with its rowdy honky-tonks and dance halls, movie theaters and eateries, prostitutes and pimps, liquor and drugs. Despite its reputation for free-flowing liquor, for us, Lyons was just another street filled with stores, bars, cleaners, and other benign establishments one might expect on a busy thoroughfare. Based on what I observed there going to and from school, the dangers of Lyons Avenue were overstated.

OUR FAMILY ATTENDED MOUNT ARARAT Baptist Church on Dan Street, just two blocks away from our house on Sumpter Street. Services at this small area church were reminiscent of those in most small Fifth Ward Baptist churches, whose preachers had been called to the ministry from blue-collar work. This church was close enough to our home that Mama would allow us to walk to Sunday services without her. She and Daddy would often set off first, arriving well in time for the devotional hour. Daddy was invited to be in the pulpit, and Mama sat near the front, her earnest piety keeping a focus on the hymns, prayers, and sermon. At thirteen and fourteen years old, I did not want to be seen sitting with my parents, so my sisters and I generally entered the sanctuary, chatted with our friends from the neighborhood, and settled into pews near the rear. Given this predictable pattern, I thought that Mama might not notice one Sunday when I failed to show up.

Dressed in my best outfit, a black and white dress made of linen-inspired synthetic that had been ironed to perfection, I walked the five blocks to dangerous Lyons Avenue, turned right, and determinedly headed toward Waco Street, looking for the church my friend had described to me. Never having walked that way alone, I was frightened by the thought of what I might encounter, but my determination to expose senseless restrictions propelled me past the streets Mama had approved for walking. Arriving at the church, I met my friend, and he escorted me into the sanctuary, where we attended a service much like those at our church on Dan Street. Conscious of the need to return home before Mama, I said goodbye immediately after the benediction and hurried home.

I was not in time. Already back at home, Mama demanded to know where I had been. The beginnings of an explanation spilled out of me. ". . . I had been invited to attend church on Lyons Avenue in broad daylight with a friend and . . . It was very safe and . . ." My mild-mannered, kind, compassionate mother struck me with a belt as she scolded me for being dishonest. At that moment, my rage and indignation matched hers. Getting a beating for attending church only proved the corruption of my parents' way of thinking: that implicit in disobedience was sinfulness and the road to ruin.

Long after that Sunday and as I started high school, I accepted unhappily the fact that my school and social life would be different from those of others, constrained by the country ways of parents who did not understand modern city life. I thought I would be bound to Mama, bound to her rules, bound to church, school, and 4432 Sumpter Street until I graduated from high school. I dutifully followed the rules and completed my first year at Wheatley with no further confrontations with Mama.

As my freshman year came to an end, I began to look forward to a summer of Hester House activity, visiting my married sisters and brothers, and keeping my nose in a book. But I soon became aware of my mother's deteriorating health. She had recently limited her outside work but took in great mounds of ironing, and despite finally having appliances that should have lightened her load, she kept a punishing schedule—cooking, cleaning, washing, and ironing every day.

Mama lived between this world and the next. She believed in "haints" because, she said, she had seen them. She also believed in omens and, having experienced premonitions, she was attentive to their warnings. When I heard her speak about such things, I was terrified by her conviction that there was more to life than what we see. She spoke to us often of frightening visions and dreams. The most beloved people in her past were her parents, Papa Richard and Mamemma, and her sister, Jim, who had died young. When she spoke of them, we sometimes had the sense that she should have been using the present tense. Mamemma died when I was two years old, but the moment and method of her death as persistently recounted by Mama almost led me to think that I remembered it myself.

Mamemma, it seems, had had a premonition of her own death. The day she died, she had carefully laid out the white Sunday clothes and black boots that she wished to be buried in. Her grandson found her body lying by the front door of her house and immediately ran to our house to inform my mother. Mama waited for no one to accompany her; she left walking to Mamemma's house to take care of her deceased mother.

Mama gave deeper meanings to many common-day occurrences and sometimes spoke of visions she had had. One day while we were living in Grapeland she had described how she watched a man approach our house. Looking out over the fields, my younger sisters and I became increasingly terrified as she told us how this stranger mysteriously and purposefully strode toward the house while she wondered who he might be and what he wanted. As he started to climb the steps of the stile to come into our yard, he vanished, she said. There was still a hint of terror in her voice as she spoke of that vision and what it might have portended.

One of the many spirituals that my mother sang both in church and around the house was "The Old Ship of Zion." That hymn speaks of a ship coming to save marooned souls and deliver them to heaven. "Get on board, get on board," the captain says. That ship is, we learn, "bound for Canaan land." Did Mama fear that she might soon be bound for Canaan, the land promised to Abraham in the Bible, which had come to symbolize for Blacks their own promised land?

Death was a constant shadow over Mama's life for all the time that I had been her daughter. Before her last three children were born, the doctor had warned her that her kidneys could not sustain further pregnancies, and even if she did not have more children, her life would be at considerable risk. She nevertheless had three more children and lived in constant fear of not surviving until the youngest of us became adults. "Just let me live long enough, Lord, for my children to be grown" was her well-known prayer. Her sensitivity to the spirit world arose not simply because of the deaths of so many whom she loved, but because, knowing that her death could come too soon, she was ever watchful for signs of the approaching end.

One day in May near the end of my first year at Wheatley, Mama didn't get out of bed. "Feeling poorly," she was weak and nauseous. Her sudden weakened state startled me. She had boiled up a gruel made of greens and cornmeal for her meals, and that morning, she directed us to prepare it and bring it to her in bed. She barely had the strength to raise herself up to take a few mouthfuls. After a number of days of seeing our mother in this state, the older children, much more knowledgeable about her medical history, called a meeting on our porch to discuss with Daddy what to do about Mama's failing health. My father was annoyed at the presumptuousness of his children to tell him how to take care of his wife. His strong will was matched by my sisters' and brothers' determination to get him to take action. From her bedroom at the front of the house, Mama could hear their loud accusations that my father was not doing enough to see that she got medical attention. The reason, they said, was his reluctance to spend money on doctors. When Mama started to cry, they all calmed down, and Daddy agreed that she should be hospitalized.

Mama was fearful of ambulances because, in Grapeland, she had associated them with death. She also was superstitious about sirens. There was no choice, however, because she could no longer walk. The ambulance was summoned to transport her to Saint Elizabeth's Hospital, a few blocks from our house. The emergency crew placed her on a stretcher, a process that took considerably longer than the brief ride to the hospital. Mama had finally agreed to go, I think, as much to keep the children from attacking Daddy as to ensure her own recovery. We all stood helpless as she was carried into the ambulance, trying not to show her our fear and sadness. They did not use a siren.

I had walked past Saint Elizabeth's Hospital every day on the way to school. A handsome white building on the corner of Yates and Lyons, it was beautifully maintained and the Catholic sisters who ran it were cheerfully accommodating but at the same time efficient and serious. Mama's doctor, Dr. Beall, had an office just across the street from the hospital. Mama had a room on the second floor and was well cared for, but that was not enough for our family. We took turns staying in her room all day and throughout the night. With the hospital only four blocks away from home, we were able to go as often as we liked.

No matter what the doctors did, her condition did not improve. At first she was lucid all the time, aware of our presence and talking with us when we visited. She could eat or drink little and would retch intermittently. She managed to suck on chipped ice to alleviate the vomiting, but this was only moderately helpful. When I visited Mama, I didn't know what to say. At first I read my schoolbooks. She would look over at me with a peaceful, interested expression, and occasionally ask me about what was happening at home. After some days, the doctors confirmed that her kidneys were failing and that she was dying from uremic poisoning. Neither dialysis nor transplantation was in wide use at the time. There was nothing that could be done. I was shocked by this news, but the noisy grief of my older sisters and stoic silence of my father and brothers suggested that no further measure was available.

The one thing they knew they had to do was bring my errant brother Chester to her side. Although keeping in regular contact with him through letters, she had not actually seen him since he ran away from home almost twenty years earlier. Now he was in jail in Chicago. Wilford and Elbert drove to Chicago, paid a fine to get him released, and brought him straight back to Houston. We had often heard Mama quietly muse, "I wonder if I'll ever see Chester again before I die." Finally, her thirty-seven-year-old son was in front of her, bald and, ironically, looking just like my father. She would have known that, for such a miracle to occur, the end must be near. Upon seeing him, she sobbed, saying little.

I had never seen my brother Chester before. Born after he had left home, I had known him only through his letters.

I'm not sure how I started writing him. It was odd to have a brother I had never met, so I decided that if I couldn't see him, at least I could write to him. I wrote to him often and he answered me. So, when he finally showed up, I felt I knew him reasonably well. He looked very different from how I had imagined him. In my imagination, he was the boy who ran away, not this older man. Over the years, he had given me lots of advice about what I should be doing, advice that he somehow could not follow himself. Never wanting to have the life my father led, working for low wages, he had gone with cousins Jack and Robert to make his fortune and landed, instead, in a life of crime and drug use.

One night shortly after Chester came home, I was told that it was my turn to stay overnight in the hospital. At fifteen years old, I was terrified that if something happened while I was there alone, I wouldn't know what to do. Mama could see my discomfort. Turning her head toward me, she said quietly, "You don't have to stay, baby, if you don't want to." I was brokenhearted. I stayed all night, giving her ice when she started to vomit. She had begun to experience hallucinations and saw animals crawling on the ceiling and phantoms standing in the room. She moaned and spoke to them throughout the night.

We were out of school for the summer and able to visit her every day. Azella, Ozella, and I, at home alone most of the time, would do the cleaning and cooking and visit Mama at the hospital. One day as we were getting dressed, Aunt Aggie called from the hospital screaming hysterically that Mama was dead. The three of us collapsed. As we were trying to decide what we should do, we received another call saying that she had not died after all. Enraged by such a callous act, we had a short time later to face the reality of her death; on June 25, 1961, a few weeks after I learned that she was gravely ill, she died.

In spite of her condition and the doctors' persistent warnings, the family was thrown into a state of shock. Fifty-five seemed too soon for anyone to die, but for Mama, whom we all regarded as saintly, it seemed especially unjust. I was confused and anxious and frightened by the reactions around me. My older sisters and our relatives wailed constantly. My father, silent and showing little emotion, became preoccupied with the funeral arrangements. The house had been transformed into the place to which Mama would never return. We were afraid to enter her bedroom and see reminders of her abrupt departure in the ambulance that she had rightly feared symbolized death. Johns Funeral Home claimed her body, and as we drove past the mortuary on Lyons Avenue, I sobbed knowing that Mama was there and we could not see her. I did not know how I would manage to get through the wake, funeral, and burial. She was to be buried on the land that Mamemma had left her children, and Uncle John, who still lived on the land, chose a site for the grave.

The first time I saw Mama at the funeral home, I was disconsolate; that moment inaugurated a period of acute personal distress that would last over a decade. Until I saw her, I could not have imagined what her death would mean to me as her youngest child. The simple woman who had refused artifice and adornment in life was heavily made up in death.

Having longed to see her in makeup and pretty clothes, I was now offended by the ruby red lipstick and frilly shroud that made her look like someone other than the mother I had known. This distortion of who she was added to the pain I was feeling. The flower-filled room was a howling place with twelve sorrowful children, each trying to imagine what life would be like without Mama. The next day, we followed the hearse on a two-hour drive to Grapeland. The long ride in the rain with the uninterrupted wailing of my sisters was agonizing. We finally arrived at Cedar Branch for the service and found the church overflowing. Reverend Thompson had come from Houston to eulogize Mama, but I could not understand anything he was saying. I tried to shut out those hymns that Mama had loved so much. Seated in front of the open casket, I thought I would not survive the service. Holding my breath to stem the tears, I began hyperventilating.

The interment in the private cemetery on Mamemma's land only heightened my distress. We entered the road to Uncle John's house and pulled up to an area to the left near the road, where the grave had been dug. It was pouring rain. The ground was muddy and the grave had begun to fill with water. When I saw that Mama was to be left in a waterlogged grave, I thought my chest would split open. Everything familiar to me seemed to be turned upside down.

Mama was buried on July 2, the day before my sixteenth birthday. I hardly took note that I turned sixteen because I was fighting to gain control over a feeling of anxiety so deep that I could not imagine my future. Every reminder of Mama's death was like a dagger: her room, Saint Elizabeth's,

Johns Funeral Home, the sound of an ambulance, the rain. I tried to concentrate on reading novels that recalled a far-gone era, anything that would help me escape the present. I visited my sisters and brothers, spending as much time as possible at Wilford's house, where I developed a special bond with his little son, Kenneth. There was something about him that Mama especially loved. He was, after all, the son of her favorite son, Wilford. At every new milestone in his development, I would think what delight Mama would have taken in what he was doing. Kept busy, I forced the days to pass, surprisingly drawing comfort from the constant dull ache in the middle of my chest. I couldn't wait for the summer to be over; I knew I needed to get back to school to deal with Mama's death.

I didn't want any reminder of the guilt that I felt. Guilt over not appreciating Mama. Guilt over being ashamed of her plainness. Guilt over not wanting to stay in the hospital with her. Guilt over having been such a pretentious brat. No matter how much I improved, she would never have a chance to see that I was the person she'd hoped I would be. Whenever I passed the funeral home, I would burst into tears. When I heard her favorite hymns in church, I became despondent. I avoided looking at the one picture we had of her. Most of all I could neither call her name nor speak of her, afraid that in doing either I would summon her spirit. Imposing an embargo on all things related to Mama and relying on my penchant for pretending to be somewhere else helped me get through the days.

As for Mama, the stranger had finally come for her. I hoped that she was peaceful. She had seen Chester again after all. Just as her wishes had willed Wilford back from Korea, they had brought Chester back to her. Her most important wish had also been satisfied: we youngest children were almost grown, and no matter what Daddy did, we would be okay. She could now go home to Canaan.

8

Black Antigone

I STARTED MY JUNIOR YEAR OF HIGH SCHOOL WITH AN ACHING feeling of emptiness and terror. For all of my teenage impatience with my mother's old-fashioned thinking and ways, Mama had been the primary anchor in my life. I was now adrift, waiting for something to replace the sense of certainty that she gave to me every day. In spite of my pretenses and affectations, I believed that, at the core, I could never be better than she. She never sought anything for herself, put her husband and children above everything, and fought mightily to live an honorable life. I did not know the half of what she had endured before I was born. There were hints and whispered conversations about my father's meanness and the children that he might have had outside our family. We thought she should be more assertive and independent, not understanding the personal fortitude needed to base her actions not on the opinions of others but on her own values. Always intent on protecting our relationship with Daddy, she refused to speak of her troubles. Learning after her death that she had been ill for over twenty years stoked my anger at my father's behavior, and Mama became a saint in my eyes. Having held on for so long, willing herself to live, and waiting for us to grow up seemed a veritably superhuman feat.

To address my profound grief and rootlessness, I looked forward to reimmersing myself in my studies and school activities. That, I thought, would take away my feelings of unworthiness. Attempting to block out the perils and problems of our ongoing poverty, I read books that enlightened me about how others had lived and coped in different times. *Anne of Green Gables* was a favorite, as aspects of Anne's life reminded me of my own dilemmas. Like me, she was talkative and a dreamer who indulged herself with affectation. But, in general, I did not so much choose the books that I read; I read what was available to me. A chivalric romance like *Ivanhoe* might seem unusual fare for a Black girl in Houston's Fifth Ward, but a hero from remote times who represented high-minded ideals drew me in because of the contrast he posed with modern-day Dixiecrats, who were wreaking terror on the Black community in the South.

I was beginning to look for models of leadership that reflected high standards and to ask myself whether I could measure up to the courage and principles they displayed. A variety of genres were commonplace fare for me and my sister Ozella, who read as extensively as I. Reading gave me an interior life that blunted the ugliness of my daily life. Every spare moment found me with a book in hand, devouring fictional characters and invented settings. I was open to any period or genre—medieval or Victorian, Renaissance or modern. Books about young girls' and women's lives held a particular allure. What kind of woman was I to become? What experiences would further shape me? Louisa May Alcott's *Little Women* was a particular favorite because of the close sisterhood it featured. What mattered most was that the authors took me to places where I didn't have to remember Mama. My resentment of Mama's suspicion of outsiders had been a constant in my childhood, but I was now able, through books and beyond, to act on my curiosity about strange and forbidden worlds, even the dangerous one so near—where whites held sway over our lives.

My family grew even more concerned about me. My sister Atherine's assertions that "something was wrong" with me and "something needed to be done" about me carried weight. Why was I reading constantly instead of doing what other children were doing? The more I read, the more I used language as a weapon—obfuscating, confusing, insulting with words that I knew most would not understand. This verbal aggression added to my sisters' concern that I was troubled. They did not tie my behavior to the grief that I nurtured to atone for my treatment of Mama or to the fact that I missed her in ways I could not yet express.

After Mama died, my sisters and I lived joylessly with our father in our sad, dark, rodent-infested rental house on Sumpter Street, fending for ourselves. His daily regimen included rising early for work and returning home at 5:00 P.M. to eat, wash up, and leave for the evening. Although he was considerably less volatile than before Mama died, he could still explode into a tirade when we did anything that was not to his liking. So accustomed to being served by my mother, he regarded not having his meals ready when he wanted them as perhaps the greatest offense. Otherwise, we had to keep the house clean, but there were few additional rules or restrictions.

In the mornings he would knock on our door before 5:00 and politely ask whether one of us would be willing to get up and cook him breakfast. This strange routine continued through the remainder of my high school years. Taking turns, one of us would rise quickly, wash up, and go to the kitchen to prepare his usual fare. We hated getting up so early but did not dare make our resentment known. One of the most puzzling dimensions of Daddy's behavior following Mama's death was that, while he always ate, he did not seem to think we needed food. Other than the breakfast foods that he preferred, he rarely bought food for us. He generally left us with only eggs, bacon, and bread in the house for our dinner.

Without any hint of grief, he quickly developed an active social life and was absent much of the time. At first, we thought he was going to evening church services, but there was more to it than that. He was enjoying the company of a particular woman. We eventually learned her identity, and every aspect of her appearance and behavior offended us because they were the opposite of Mama's modesty.

Miss Eula Mae was a coquette with a high-pitched giggle that almost anything could provoke. She wore colorful outfits and makeup that seemed inappropriate for a middle-aged woman. At the same time, my father's behavior in her presence was most off-putting; he appeared inordinately pleased with this silly woman.

After Daddy left for work, we would get ready for school with the house all to ourselves. Even in high school we had very meager wardrobes, so we swapped clothes whenever we could, mixing the pieces to make it appear that we had more than three outfits each. Afraid to tell Daddy what kinds of clothes high school required, we had to avoid joining any clubs that required special dress. Fortunately, the drama club had no need of uniforms or equipment; costumes were available for actors.

I don't remember when I first discovered that the theater was my way out. Intense, therapeutic, and wholly absorbing, it became a hiding place and refuge from my confusion and despair. After I joined Phillis Wheatley's Stagecrafters Club, theater became an all-consuming activity. As a member of the club, I was required to participate in every activity: building and painting sets, rehearsing plays, and the manifold other assignments needed to stage a production. Sadly, given Mama's strict rules about going straight home after school, my immersion in theater was possible only after her death.

The students active in the Stagecrafters Club looked forward to the end of the school day, when we would all retire to our drama teacher Miss Lillie's classroom or the auditorium. There we would rehearse our lines, work on sets and props, and prepare costumes for whatever show was in production. *The Glass Menagerie* was the play of choice in my junior year.

My sisters Azella and Ozella, a year ahead of me, had roles in some of the plays. There we were, the three of us together, bereft and throwing ourselves into this wonderfully engrossing activity, making a new home.

I was relieved to have my sisters participate in the same activities I did. Ozella, the taller and more academically oriented of the two, was similar to me in interests. This gave rise to a healthy competition between us, although she had stricter limits on what she would and would not do. I was reasonably compliant in following requirements, but she followed her own rules. For example, she got into quite a bit of trouble because she refused to participate in gym class. While her explanation was the lack of a gym uniform, I thought she simply didn't like the activity. Azella's personality was quite different; gregarious, lighthearted, and likable, she made friends easily and gave no hint of resistance to adult guidance. She drew praise for her beautiful singing voice and, after high school, she performed professionally, singing R & B tunes in nightclubs. Though very different from each other, the twins tended to be unified in their judgment of me: I was spoiled.

We three were of one mind, however, about our captivating drama teacher. Although we called her Miss Lillie, Vernell Lillie was married with children. It was a common convention to call all women "Miss"; the two-syllable "Mrs." was almost never used in our community. Miss Lillie had grown up in Houston and attended Dillard University in Louisiana. She lived in Pleasantville, a small middle-class Black community down Market Street, not far from Wheatley, with her husband, Richard, and her two young daughters, Charisse and Marsha. Though less than five feet tall, she was a striking presence because of her studied theatrical movements and ever-present stiletto pumps. With her deep, resonant voice, she crisply enunciated every syllable and paused at certain moments for maximum impact. In spite of her relaxed manner and a sense of humor that made her amiable and approachable, her overall mien was elegant and even regal. Miss Lillie strode commandingly around the classroom or on the stage in full performance mode, gesturing to emphasize certain points about the plays she had us study. Reading dialogue, she sounded as accomplished as anyone we saw on television; a minute change in inflection or the slightest movement could draw our attention and clarify meaning. I was grateful to have such a fascinating person as a teacher.

In drama I could be anything I chose to be. Under Miss Lillie's guidance, I could become anyone a playwright created and be cast in any work, no matter the plot or the race of the characters. We read plays from across the spectrum of world drama: Shakespeare and Ibsen, Tennessee Williams and Eugène Ionesco, Sophocles and Hansberry. Few high school students of drama could be getting a broader sampling of plays and roles than I and my friends in Houston's Fifth Ward.

Miss Lillie singled me out in class as someone who could play serious roles. What had been a peculiarity of my personality—a manner of speaking that set me apart from my friends and family—finally became an asset. I could perform a variety of characters, matching my speech to the needs of the genre and era. I learned to mimic different speech patterns because this activity required neither money nor anyone's permission. After having been ridiculed for my country looks and manner of speech, improving my speech gave me the means to think I could be better than those who made fun of me. My mannerisms matched my speech as I grew increasingly dramatic in my gestures, creating the impression that I was always acting out a role. In addition, like Anne of Green Gables, I unilaterally changed my name, adding an "e" to my first name and "ne" to my middle name. "Ruthe Jeanne Stubblefield" seemed more fitting for the persona I sought to create.

I relished this opportunity to play a variety of characters. Taking on one role after another, I hoped that entering the psyches of these characters might help me better understand myself. If I were remembered for any role I played at Wheatley, it would be for that of Sophocles's Antigone. Although the drama's stilted poetic language was a challenge, I brought to this tragic heroine all my sadness and grief from my mother's death. I understood and admired Antigone's courage taking on the power of the state to defend an important principle. Reciting the brave words of protest she spoke in the face of Creon's power prompted me to think of what it would mean for me to live a life of honor and duty. I began to understand that I would need to develop greater personal independence and courage for the life I wanted to live. Much later, as my career as a college president developed, I came to understand how important this early recognition had been. I was later to make pivotal choices that originated in the ideal of personal strength shown by Antigone.

We also mounted Ionesco's *The Bald Soprano*. One of my best friends from high school who later followed me to Dillard, Noah Kemp, played opposite me in this absurdist drama.

Like me, he relished the author's non sequiturs and strange characters. The surprising and dissonant effect of the improbably juxtaposed dialogue was a feast for all of us in the drama club. Surprisingly, our Fifth Ward audiences, understanding little about this play, enjoyed the production. Its lines kept us in laughter; for many years Noah and I would gleefully return to our memorized Ionesco repartee.

Through acting out different roles, I discovered that I was not separated from the rest of the world's experience of and reaction to humor and tragedy. Furthermore, showing these characters to our friends and community was gratifying and empowering for all of us drama students. Stepping onto a stage and playing characters so removed from our lives was in some ways a heroic act. These would be the only theatrical experiences many of us would ever have. The applause that greeted every performance was reassuring and, at times, uplifting. After weeks memorizing lines and rehearsing, it was difficult to leave roles that had taken on a meaning and connection to my life. Had I eventually found the character that suited me ideally, I might have happily disappeared completely from the world.

Living with and caring for the characters in our productions led me to develop additional affectations that must have been troubling for those observing me outside the theater. I continued to project a theatrical persona to replace the wounded self that could not cope with Mama's absence. Desperately parodying theatrical behavior, I began calling everyone "*Dahhh* . . . ling," with the first syllable elaborately inflected. My natural loquaciousness, having been a nuisance for my family ever since I decided to learn every word in the dictionary, became even more frenetic and my behavior even more imperious. I routinely ridiculed my sisters and was quick to point out others' imperfections.

Yet a variety of positive activities grew out of these affectations. I entered debate contests, where I could use my stylized speech to advantage. Commissioned to portray a character who talked about how glorious Wheatley was during halftime at football games, I did not blandly read a script, I acted out the words to stunned fans. I deployed the same character when Miss Lillie secured me a regular spot on KYOK, a local Black radio station. In my weekly segment, I was Ruthe Stubblefield, a Wheatley student who was a gossipy character reporting on and announcing upcoming school happenings. Within a year of Mama's death, I had gone from grief and mourning to a frenzied array of activities.

My reputation as an actress was growing, thanks to Miss Lillie. She looked for opportunities for me to perform a one-woman show based on my radio persona. Of the scores of activities that I participated in, my father never attended a single one. Considering his parenting role over, he showed no interest in what any of us girls were doing. He went on with his life—now preaching in small churches—and left us to ours. Though disappointed in his attitude, we knew the disadvantages of having his full attention; our movements would have been severely circumscribed had he chosen to commit to a full parental role.

My older sisters and brothers recognized what was happening and eagerly became surrogate parents. Wilford, especially, always came to see me perform, encouraged my speech and drama activities, and paid for the necessary incidentals. I understood more and more why my mother had loved this son so deeply. Now with a schoolteacher wife and two children, he could have left us on our own. Further, working in a local oil refinery under discriminatory conditions that he was protesting, he did not have much financial flexibility. Kind beyond measure, he understood that, now that my mother was gone, he needed to be present in our lives even with his own family demands. No other person except my mother would ever have a more positive and indelible effect on my character and on what I sought to become in my adult and professional life. Wilford's concern for others greatly moved me; I wanted to be like him, but how could I move beyond my juvenile antics to such a state? I hoped that my education would show me the way.

Outside of school, Miss Lillie found numerous ways of exposing me to the arts. She would take me with her daughters in her small Hillman car to museums and cultural events in the area. I could not believe that Blacks could move so freely around the city and state, enter debate contests and go to museums and plays. I saw more of the city and region in my final two years of high school than I had seen previously in all my years in Houston; I had been imprisoned in the two square miles framed by Liberty Road to the north and Market Street to the south, Jensen Avenue to the west and Lockwood Avenue to the east.

I got to know Miss Lillie's family well and was amazed at how inviting and generous they all were. Marsha and Charisse, both still in elementary school the year I met them, treated the older stagecrafters like siblings. Mr. Lillie was mild-mannered, tall, and handsome, with a jazz musician's smoothness in speech and movements. Always with a knowing, beneficent twinkle in his eye, he was tolerant of our youthful behavior. The fact that he supported what Miss Lillie was doing and was a loving father showed me again how deficient my own father's parenting had been. I realized that Daddy had not given me a fraction of what Mr. Lillie appeared to give his daughters in love and support. Daddy was brave, determined, and proud, it is true, but his own tragic childhood made close, loving relationships difficult. He kept us together under one roof until adulthood, but he saw his obligation merely in those terms. The Lillie family was a new model for me. Miss Lillie helping us drama students far beyond what was required by the school district and her entire family embracing us made me think about my responsibility to others beyond my own family. I began to commit to future service to our larger community and to those who might have even less than I.

At home, I never talked about Mama. I didn't need to summon her; she was everywhere. In everything. A constant presence within a haunting absence. Her exhortations continued to guide us. Her work ethic pushed us to do more and do better. Going to church was another balm for my grief. There I could hear Mama's hymns and collapse in tears without anyone associating my actions with grief; the congregation most likely thought I was merely "getting happy." Behind those church tears was a redoubt of anger, pain, and hurt in my hundred-pound frame.

The more acting I did, the more difficult I became for

everyone around me. I pushed people away with a well-honed trenchant sarcasm that usually derided their intelligence and used language I knew my peers would not understand. In contrast to the Black dialect that everyone around me spoke—eliding syllables, performing surgery on consonantal endings, and misusing tenses, I was intent on speaking the King's English. I relished neologisms, multisyllabic words, and any vocabulary that could draw attention to my verbal prowess. Miss Lillie spoke to me about my erratic and frequently outlandish behavior but with such patience and understanding that her advice hardly had an impact. After sixteen years of Mama's watchfulness, Miss Lillie was now watching me, ready to chastise me when needed. And she did.

Among Wheatley's small faculty, there were many teachers of exceptional talent. Teaching was one of the few professional jobs a Black person could hold. Our teachers had, therefore, overcome a high hurdle and were among the most conscientious, able, and intelligent Blacks of their generation. The English Department was especially strong, with Mr. Gideon Saunders, a superb teacher with effeminate ways who was a frequent foil for student jokes, Miss Eddye Bird, and Miss Wilma Smith. Their insistence that we learn standard language usage might have annoyed most students, but it helped us develop exceptional skills. Outside the Wheatley building, though, most students reverted to a Fifth Ward lingua franca that bore no resemblance to Standard English. Except me. I defiantly spoke in a way that was identical to how I spoke in my English classes. I was not troubled by the ribbing that I took: "She's so seditty!" "She speaks too proper!"

"She thinks she's better than anybody else!" My years as the runt of the litter had prepared me well for defying the urge to conform.

In spite of my idiosyncratic tastes and behavior, overall, I was making friends, participating in school activities, and, I thought, slowly recovering from my mother's death. I also fell in love that year. I had met and started seeing a boy named Harry Richmond the summer following my junior year. My first boyfriend, he was generally able to tolerate my odd behavior even when he seemed not to understand it. We were in different social groups; I was identified with the egghead group while he was a basketball player like my brothers. Handsome, athletic, and smooth, he was known as a lady's man and people whispered that he had actually gotten a girl pregnant in junior high school. One day, he approached me and we started talking. I was surprised by his intelligence, intensity, and affability. Flattered by his attention, I was also surprisingly comfortable in his presence.

Harry lived with his single mother several blocks from us but in a much nicer house. At the end of the school day, he seemed to make an effort to find me and walk with me. Over the weeks, we became close friends. Mama and Daddy had never allowed us to go to sock hops at Hester House, and if a boy had called me at home, it would have created a ruckus. Having no experience talking to boys or dating, I didn't know how to handle Harry's attention. Because I had no mother at home, the principal of Wheatley feared that I was vulnerable to Harry's well-known exploits. It was rumored that school staff had threatened Harry that if he behaved improperly toward me, he would face repercussions. I didn't dare ask him if this was true, and I decided it hardly mattered. My seven brothers were enough of a deterrent to any misbehavior.

I enjoyed Harry's company and was grateful for his attention. Still, feeling self-conscious about my clothes and my appearance, I couldn't imagine anyone as popular and handsome as Harry being attracted to me. I initially kept him at a distance, but by the time my junior year drew to an end, I was completely smitten. I relied on my feelings for him to stanch fears about what my life would become now that Mama was gone.

Harry started coming to our house and, to my surprise, my father did not throw him out. When we weren't together, we were on the telephone until late at night, talking about unremarkable things. I was often confused about where our friendship might ultimately lead but, in spite of his history, Harry made no effort to coax me into a sexual relationship. He was attentive and loving, making it clear that he cared deeply for me. His presence not only filled my life and helped me get over my mother's death but also gave me a growing sense of self-confidence which, up until then, I had only pretended to possess. As the summer of 1962 ended and I began my senior year, I knew that I was about to accomplish something Mama would have been proud of.

That year I was asked to run for Miss Wheatley, the school beauty queen. I lost to Eloise Curtis but, as the first runner-up, I was a member of the royal court and had to purchase a long dress, hat, gloves, and shoes in Wheatley's colors—purple and white—to wear in a parade. I called Wilford and asked for the money. Without hesitation, he gave it to me.

At the beginning of my senior year, I became caught up in my anxiety about what might happen once I graduated. Miss Lillie was convinced that I could be a professional actress. As the time approached for me to think about college, she helped me identify universities with serious theater programs. She considered Iowa State an excellent choice, and I applied there not having any idea where Iowa was. Having studied at Dillard University in New Orleans, she advised me to apply there as well. One of a number of Black colleges affiliated with the Methodist Church, Dillard was founded in 1869 as Straight University. It later merged with New Orleans University to form Dillard. By 1963 it had become a liberal arts college whose purpose was to transform first-generation Black college students into profession-bound graduates capable of proving to whites that Blacks were ready for and deserving of equality as American citizens. Universities in Houston or elsewhere in Texas, still roiling from the first efforts at integration, were not deemed suitable for outspoken Black students. The South was not ready for a Black Antigone.

HARRY AND I DRIFTED APART as the year wore on. I was immersed in planning for my future, but he seemed not to have plans. I felt awkward about discussing college plans with him because they would inevitably bring to mind my leaving him behind in Houston. Gradually, he seemed to disappear, and I soon heard he was seeing another girl. Though I had been aware of a strain between us, I was heartbroken that he had another girlfriend. There was nothing I could do except throw myself even deeper into my work with the theater. I also managed to keep up my work in other classes and, since my grades were exceptional, I knew that I would graduate somewhere near the top of my class.

As senior prom approached, I realized that I would not be going with Harry, as I had once expected. When Ricky Cassell, president of the student council, asked me to be his date, I agreed. Carolyn Lewis, a girl with interests similar to mine, also unusual among Wheatley students, was my best friend. She had an acerbic sense of humor, was very articulate, and appreciated the arts and literature. We decided to double-date for the prom. I called Wilford again and asked him for money for a gown.

Thanks to Miss Lillie, Dillard offered me admission and I received a generous scholarship from a local foundation. I was astonished that I was actually going to college. One hurdle remained; I needed my father's permission. How would he react when I told him I wanted to go to college in New Orleans? Terrified, I rehearsed my conversation with him and finally got the nerve to ask. "Daddy, I got a scholarship to go to Dillard University in New Orleans. Can I go?" Expecting a no, I was not surprised by his response: "Yes, as long as it doesn't cost me one red penny!" I knew attending Dillard would be a severe squeeze with no help from Daddy, but I told no one that he had refused to help me. I hoped that, once I got to college, he might relent. What was most important to me was that he had given me permission to go.

The thirty-fifth commencement exercises of Phillis Wheat-

ley High School took place on May 30, 1963, at the Music
Hall in downtown Houston. Printed in the middle of the
purple-fringed programs was the theme, "Scholarship, Character, Service." I was listed as number two in my class, after William Grover, a math whiz. My name appeared in the program
as Ruthe Jeanne Stubblefield, the alter ego I had created for
myself.

As the ceremony got under way, Mr. Moseley's band
played the processional, Mendelssohn's "War March of the
Priests," and a pastor from Antioch Church gave the invo-
cation. After the girls' choir sang, we settled in to hear the
commencement address by a faculty member from Texas
Southern University, a Black college in Houston. The recognition that here, finally, was what Mama had been fighting to
stay alive for swept over me. I had succeeded in every way
she could have wished for me. She would never know that
the values she had taught me through lectures, upright living,
and stern restrictions had taken hold. I could not suppress
the tears and wept uncontrollably.

Word first passed among the students, then the teachers,
then the crowd that I was crying. Soon my friends, teachers,
and family were in tears, too. Embarrassed to have fallen
apart, I dreaded having to walk onto the stage for my diploma.
All the tears that I had held in over the prior months came
pouring out, as if I were still standing before Mama's coffin,
acknowledging my loss for the very first time. Embarrassed, I
took my diploma and hurried back to my seat. After the ceremony, my sisters and brothers pressed around asking me
what was wrong. I could not speak. I could not tell them how
inconsolably broken I was that Mama could not see me grad-

uate. The same feeling of regret and longing has overwhelmed me again at every important moment of my life, including when I became president of Smith and president of Brown University. I could never fully enjoy any accomplishment without my mother's presence.

9

Community

I SPENT THE SUMMER OF 1963 VISITING TEACHERS AND FAMILY members, planning my trip to New Orleans, and working for my former teacher, Mrs. Caraway, who had hired me intermittently since I'd graduated from eighth grade to clean her house and do odd jobs. For a child from Sumpter Street, the Caraway home was luxurious. Though less than ten miles from our Fifth Ward neighborhood, the Black Third Ward, where the Caraways lived, had an upscale reputation. Aspiring Blacks moved to this neighborhood of neat rows of brick bungalows and two-story houses. Owning a residence made of bricks was considered the pinnacle of Black wealth. The Caraways' bungalow was not made of brick, but I was still astonished that Blacks could live as they did.

Located on a street of well-tended middle-class dwellings, their three-bedroom house was clean, tastefully furnished, and ready for the rare overnight guest. The formal living room displayed a collection of antique glass and porcelain figurines and had a sofa and chairs upholstered in an off-white damask fabric that matched the chairs in the adjoining formal dining room, where a china cabinet stood proudly displaying prized dishes. A center hallway extended from the living room to the rear of the house, where the Caraways had remodeled a porch into a den with bookcases, a large red sofa, and his and hers chairs.

Having no children of their own, Mr. and Mrs. Caraway treated me as a surrogate child. They looked after me, helped me earn money, advised me about what I might face in life, and provided an example of what middle-class life might hold for me if I graduated from college. The days I worked for them were ten percent work and ninety percent social. When I completed my assigned chores, Mrs. Caraway and I would go shopping, have lunch in one of her favorite restaurants (either El Chico's or Luby's Cafeteria), visit her friends or family, or stop by Mr. Caraway's dry-cleaning business. Lunches involved traditional southern dishes: okra, cornbread dressing, roasted chicken, corn, sautéed squash, and sweet iced tea. Increasingly, we were drawn to Mexican fare: cheese enchiladas, tacos, rice, refried beans, and tortillas. The days were exhausting, not so much from the cleaning as from Mrs. Caraway's intense and hurried pace. Hurry with the cleaning, Ruth, before it gets too hot. Hurry with lunch to get to Walter Pye's department store before a certain salesperson gets off. Hurry so that I can get back to get Finis's dinner ready.

Mrs. Caraway's sister, Dorothy Peters, dissimilar to her in many ways but as close as an identical twin, was also childless. She eventually became a member of our odd trio—two older women, confirmed shopaholics with indulgent husbands, and a teenager. Everywhere we went, passersby, salespeople, waiters, and shop owners marveled at the intensity of the sisters' loud, quarrelsome interaction as they rushed through stores looking for bargains. The older of the two, Mrs. Caraway treated Mrs. Peters like a child, dictating what she should do, while Mrs. Peters usually retorted like a rebellious teenager. Broad-shouldered and loud even when she whispered, Mrs. Caraway, so intent on teaching all of her students to be proper, discreet, and orderly ("Act like you got some sense," she would say), generated the kind of fanfare that accomplished the exactly opposite impression. In spite of their squabbles, the sisters were devoted to each other and, during the summer, spent a significant part of the day together shopping in every store where they thought they could capture top-quality clothing at reduced prices. During these escapades, I observed patiently, amused not merely by their antics but also by the wide-eyed stares of white salespeople who did not know what to make of these noisy Black women on shopping sprees.

Shopping with Mrs. Caraway was an eye-opening experience. She not only purchased items she needed in great quantity but purchased things she did not need in great quantity. Her closets were filled with new shoes and clothing that, with tags still attached, she had never worn. Well known to the salespeople in her favorite stores, she would identify items and, when the prices went down, they would put them aside for her. She was among the best-dressed teachers at E. O. Smith, her clothes reflecting her expensive tastes.

When I visited the Caraways, I would occasionally spend the night. Invariably, I would see unemptied shopping bags from previous expeditions stacked in the spare bedrooms. It was not unusual for her to buy the same item in a number of colors. Sadly, I have now taken to doing the same.

Mr. Caraway didn't get home from work until late in the day, and in the summer Mrs. Caraway had a lot of time to devote to her person and her acquisitions once the house was clean and his meals prepared. Her household goal was to eliminate in record time any potential for bacteria. Devoted to strong-smelling solvents that she deemed effective in abolishing germs by the force of their fumes, she relied on ammonia, Clorox, Bon Ami, and Pine-Sol. I was an inexpensive but effective assistant in her mission.

The stark contrast between Mrs. Caraway—tall, strong, and assertive—and Mr. Caraway—small in stature and reticent in speech—was striking. It was entertaining to see them together, and I wondered how their improbable union had occurred. While he was barely noticeable, her bearing and manner of speaking made her unforgettable from the moment I first met her. Mrs. Caraway spoke with a peculiar combination of precise elocution interspersed with malapropisms and crude vernacular terms. Her tendency to enunciate with great care while mispronouncing words made for comic relief in her classes and caused children to mimic her distinctive style of speaking. Long after leaving her classes, they could be heard talking about how she called them "cheerin" instead of "children."

Despite the incongruity of her language usage, Mrs. Caraway's mission was to be stylish in all dimensions of her person. In addition to her exceptional wardrobe, she paid considerable attention to her face and had a vast assortment of mysterious creams and atomizers arrayed on her dresser and in her bathroom. Gifted with flawless dark skin, she applied her makeup with great deftness and faithfully had her hair styled and her nails manicured every week. No one else I knew had such luxuries. Her thin hair made it difficult to hold a style, so when wigs became acceptable and ubiquitous, she would occasionally substitute one for her own pressed and curled hair. Still, she was an icon of glamour in my eyes. The fact that Mrs. Caraway could use all that she earned to maintain her face, hair, nails, and wardrobe in no way dimmed my admiration.

On the days that I visited or worked for her, Mrs. Caraway would sometimes prepare my favorite lunch: tuna salad with shredded carrots, diced apples, celery, onion, diced hard-boiled eggs, mayonnaise, and Worcestershire sauce. In the dining nook adjoining the kitchen, she set the small table with place mats and silver. Over lunch, she talked about what lay ahead for me. She did not restrain herself from offering advice. I had never had a talk from my mother or father about the facts of life, and Mrs. Caraway provided the information I needed in the form of uniquely colorful, if crude, warnings. "Ruth, don't you let no nappy-headed nigga stand in the way of what you need to do, you hear me?" In spite of her remonstrances, she was a big fan of my high school boyfriend, Harry, who virtually everyone else thought to be somewhat thuggish and certainly bad for me. I suspected that her affinity for Harry was based largely on the fact that he was fair and did not have nappy hair.

In spite of Mrs. Caraway's racial pride and her devotion to all of us, it was quite evident that she had been cursed with the self-hatred that was so prevalent in the Black community at that time. She considered nappy hair horrifying, dark skin unfortunate, large lips laughable, and thick nostrils "niggerish." I marveled that someone so intelligent could be so misguided in matters of racial pride and identity. Even more remarkable was the fact that she would openly express such aversions to her students, most of whom were, like me, dark and nappy headed.

Yet, when it came to helping students, shade of skin and hair texture seemed not to matter. For example, my niece Elma and I were both in Mrs. Caraway's class in the ninth grade, and it was clear to me that Mrs. Caraway preferred Elma because she had less kinky hair and lighter skin than I. She praised Elma for her intelligence, her poise, and her good looks—all of which were valid compliments—and pronounced frequently that Elma would be far more successful than I in life because of these features. I was not offended by Mrs. Caraway's remarks. I made light of her idiosyncrasies, attributing them to her generation and age. Besides, I admired my niece Elma just as much as Mrs. Caraway did. It was not until I got to college and studied the work of people like Frantz Fanon that I came to understand the extent of the self-hatred engendered within the Black community as a consequence of slavery and the ongoing racial discrimination in the United States. In effect, Mrs. Caraway turned her scorn upon herself, because her skin was very dark, and her hair was as nappy as that of any of the students she accused of possessing such features.

Miss Lillie, Mrs. Caraway, and another teacher, Miss Marie Farnsworth, were concerned about my not having suitable clothes for college. Mrs. Caraway was a larger woman, whose clothes would not fit my hundred-pound body; Miss Lillie was considerably shorter than I; but Miss Farnsworth was fit and slim. I knew her much less well than I knew Mrs. Caraway and Miss Lillie, but she was an excellent teacher whom I admired not only for her intelligence and trenchant wit but also for her stylish dress.

One day Miss Farnsworth invited me to her home in Third Ward to help with cleaning. She lived not far from Mrs. Caraway but in a much fancier community, overlooking the bayou. In contrast with the large traditional mansions occupied by the wealthiest Blacks of that era, her home was contemporary in design. When I arrived, she invited me to look through her closet, which was even more extensively stocked than Mrs. Caraway's. She had sorted through her wardrobe to identify what might be appropriate for a seventeen-year-old, and she insisted that I take the items she had chosen. I was embarrassed and moved by her generosity. I could not understand how she'd guessed that I probably didn't have clothes to take to college. Had Miss Lillie told her? That she gave me exceptionally stylish clothes she had purchased for herself made the gift even more meaningful. One of the ensembles was a black and beige striped two-piece outfit that I am wearing in my freshman yearbook picture at Dillard. Each time I see the photograph, I remember this teacher's generosity and am prompted to action as an educator that extends beyond circumscribed duties to the full breadth of students' needs.

That summer Ozella married Denver Raymond and they were living with Denver's parents not far from Sumpter Street. Ozella had graduated the year before and started college at Texas Southern University, only to drop out after one semester. She had had a big row with Daddy about his not helping to pay her tuition but, with her marriage, that was now a moot point. Daddy believed not only that a child should be independent at age eighteen but that once married, at whatever age, she should be financially independent. Azella was the only other child still at home. With markedly different interests, she and I went in different directions as I prepared to leave home.

Our ever-expanding extended family now had scores of nieces and nephews scattered throughout the Houston area. Not only were we siblings close, perpetuating the constant sibling interaction that our parents had modeled for us, but nieces and nephews were also choosing friendships within the family over others. I would occasionally spend the night with my married siblings and their families. After living with us for several years before Mama died, Nora had remarried and moved out of our home with Crystal, her six-year-old from her first marriage. I often visited her to find food and to see Crystal, who was more like a sister to us than a niece. Nora and I did not get along well when she lived with us but, once she moved, I began to rely on her more as an older sister. Her new husband, Nathaniel Wilson, was very kind to us, never complaining that we were constantly around and underfoot.

We were welcome in all of their homes. Ruben and Novella had two small boys, and Ruben, now a fireman, was working the odd fireman's shifts, which made it difficult to catch him. I enjoyed babysitting his boys whenever I could. Novella was a wonderful cook, and we always found delicious cakes when we visited their home. Although Atherine still lived in La Marque, I tried to spend a week with her during the summer. Her children were fourteen, twelve, and nine; Donald, the middle child, was especially garrulous and constantly misbehaving. I enjoyed the small-town life of La Marque and her efforts to control her three children and their many activities. She had been my babysitter when I was a toddler, but she had no similar assistance with her own children. Mama had been fortunate, I thought, to have older children to assist her, and I wondered how I might eventually manage if I had children.

Clarence was finishing up his undergraduate program at Prairie View A&M University, but Arnold and Albert were also married and living close by. I spent most of my time with Wilford and his wife, Irma. They had two children, Brenda Kay and Kenneth, aged four and three, respectively. I loved being in Wilford and Irma's home, and from time to time I babysat and helped Irma with chores. Both she and Wilford were easygoing and permissive as parents. Mama had been very attached to Kenneth and, recalling her fondness for him, I considered being with him a special treat. Brenda was precocious and talkative, and easy to take care of. With Mama gone, I considered Wilford and Irma more like parents and Brenda and Kenneth like younger siblings.

Elbert, Erma Mae, and their three daughters had relocated to Third Ward's Anita Street, adjacent to the University of Houston campus. I would occasionally stay at their home, where my niece Elma and I, the same age, had the opportunity to catch up on each other's activities. As residents of Third Ward, Elbert and Erma Mae's girls matriculated at Jack Yates High School so, after E. O. Smith, Elma and I were no longer in the same classes. Elbert, ever the upstanding and stalwart oldest of us, continued to model the highest aspirations and standards. He had become a minister like my father, but the authenticity of his "calling" was never questioned. Erma Mae was a fashionable first lady of the church; she had attained her goal for the family: to advance to middle-class status and to ensure that all of her girls were educated.

Daddy was not much of a presence that summer. Though he was faithful to his responsibility to be home every night, his companion, Miss Eula Mae, occupied a good deal of his time. Despite the fact that she was quite the opposite of Mama, we had no good reason to dislike her, and we eventually placed all of our resentment on our father for abandoning Mama so easily. With Ozella gone and my impending departure, we wondered why he did not marry. But he appeared content to "keep company" with Miss Eula Mae indefinitely, although we had the impression that she was intensely interested in the subject. He asked no questions about Dillard, ventured no advice, offered no financial assistance. He thought that, at seventeen, I should be independent, working and taking care of myself. Remembering how he tried to prevent my sister Atherine from leaving the farm after she married, I was grateful enough that he did not oppose my plans. Although his seeming indifference to my circumstances annoyed my sisters and brothers, particularly Wilford and Atherine, they, too, knew there was nothing to be done after he had failed to support Ozella's en-rollment at Texas Southern University. I was on my own.

Daddy's attitude did not dampen my resolve because I knew how much strong support I had from many others. There were all of my brothers and sisters—including Chester who, after Mama's death, continued his mysterious, distant, and probably criminal ways but always helped me when he could. None of my siblings was well off at that point, but they were all securely employed. Two years after my mother's death, we were closer than ever, and my teachers were members of my extended family. I knew that I could count on the Lillies and Caraways in particular for financial help in times of difficulty. They had done so much for me already. Not only had they invited me into their homes and their families but they had exposed me to opportunities and experiences I would not have known without them, experiences that greatly increased my ambition and aspirations. I felt willing to test myself at Dillard primarily because they had helped me see that I had the potential to achieve beyond what my personal circumstances might imply. I knew I needed them to remain a continuous part of my life. I silently made that promise to myself. The best way to show how much I cared for them and appreciated their help was to succeed at Dillard, and beyond.

PART THREE

The World

10

Fair Dillard

ON THE LONG TRAIN RIDE FROM HOUSTON TO NEW Orleans, I reflected on the surprising turn that my life had taken. I had often mused about whether I would ever be able to go to college. I had received Worthing Foundation and KYOK scholarships as well as one from Dillard so, at last, I was on my way, fulfilling my dream of crossing the economic and racial barriers that had marked my family's history. I had been unfamiliar with the Worthing Scholarship before I learned that I had received one. The notion that a generous person had decided to provide scholarships for Blacks in that era surprised and comforted me. Wheatley teachers had undoubtedly appealed to the foundation on my behalf. So many organizations, individuals, and family members supporting me spurred me to do whatever I could to measure up to their confidence in me.

I wished that Mama had lived to see me board the train to New Orleans. To see the delight on her face would have made me the happiest of all travelers. I thought back over the two eventful and transformative years since her death and prayed that the coming years in an unfamiliar place and context would not cause my sorrow to overtake me again. I wondered how I would manage without the constant presence of my large family and amazing teachers. I didn't worry about being away from the friends I had made in high school; I was ready to find new friends, from whom I would learn a good deal more about the world and, possibly, myself.

At first, these thoughts, and many others, kept me from appreciating the passing scenery, so different from any that I had known. The eerie beauty of the Atchafalaya wetlands as the train left Texas alerted me that I was about to encounter a world vastly different from any I had known. That difference would not be manifested simply in the swampy landscape; I was entering a phase of my life that would reshape my sense of who I was and who I could ultimately become.

Finally, arriving in New Orleans at night, I shared a taxi to the campus with another student from Houston, Sandra Butler. Exhausted and apprehensive, we made our way to get our room assignments and collect our keys. When I first saw the campus lit up in the dark, I was pleased but couldn't tell much from the shadowy outlines. My first train ride, my first time away from my family, my first time in another state, my first ride in a taxi, my first time on a college campus—that was enough for one day. I hastily made up my bed, slipped in between the stiffly pressed sheets given to me, and fell fast asleep.

WHEN I AWOKE EARLY THE next morning and left the dormitory to find breakfast, I could hardly believe my eyes. Before me was one of the most beautiful campuses that I could have imagined. From the entrance on Gentilly Boulevard near Elysian Fields, the campus was dominated by an expansive promenade of majestic oaks, setting off the stark white-columned buildings. The impression was of a large antebellum plantation. At the front of the campus, on either side of this magnificent avenue of oaks were two buildings, Stern and Rosenwald Halls, named for two benefactors of the university. The center promenade was transected by walkways giving access to less important buildings and warning that we must not step off the walk onto the perfectly manicured and maintained lawn. Strategically placed benches along the walkway afforded students the opportunity to congregate without disturbing the grass. I thought of the contrast with "buzzards' roost" in Grapeland.

I had not heard about and was not prepared for the formality of the campus. The students moving across this scenic postcard disrupted my early morning reflections. I imagined them to be as happy as I with the pristine setting, whose formal architecture and landscape design led it to be added to the National Register of Historic Places several decades later. In truth, Dillard's campus landscape tended to dominate most references to the university. Even the school song celebrated the beauty of the white buildings against the verdant expanse of the grounds:

> *Fair Dillard, gleaming white and spacious green,*
> *We love thy every blade and tree . . .*

At a time when opportunities for Blacks to feel proud were still rare, the pride of place that the campus inspired fueled my growing sense of entitlement to equality and the determination to prove myself worthy of it.

I settled into my comfortable room in Straight Hall, the freshman dorm, without much anxiety in spite of the loneliness that I felt much of the time. I shared a room with Sandra, my companion from the train ride from Houston. I thought it extraordinary that she and I would be on the same train until I learned how this coincidence had come about. She was the niece of Wheatley's principal, Mr. William Moore, who had requested that she room with me. He must have known that Sandra and I were polar opposites, but that was precisely the point. I had graduated at the top of my class, was a serious student and a "good" girl. Sandra was an adequate student with little interest in academics. She was, however, fun loving and socially experienced. I had not known her well in high school and soon recognized that my biggest challenge of the year might be managing my relationship with her.

Sandra was open and friendly, confident and sassy. Away from her uncle and ready to have a good time, she poured her energy into getting to know people and sampling the nightlife of New Orleans. Pragmatic and determined, I was focused on learning all I could, excelling in my classes, and getting a good night's sleep. Once I started studying, Sandra would begin making noise: talking to me or other friends, wandering the halls, drinking, anything, it seemed, to distract me, prevent me from sleeping, or awaken me. Soon I was frustrated and unhappy with our being roommates. I wanted to enjoy the newfound luxury of quiet and solitude. Sandra's loud presence was reminiscent of all the years I had to accommodate my sisters in our cramped rooms.

I found my classes less stimulating than I had expected. I had thought that college would be more challenging but, forgetting how hard Wheatley teachers had worked to provide advanced material to me, I discovered that some of the classes at Dillard were disappointingly similar to my high school courses. Biology and English were my favorite subjects, but mostly because the professors were inspiring and seemed concerned that I excel. Still determined to become an actress, I enrolled in Drama 203—Dramatic Interpretation—with Mr. Greenhoe. I soon realized that a number of students involved in theater at Dillard had considerable experience and I recognized that I had much to do to prove myself as an actor. Hearing their sophisticated repartee peppered with allusions that I could not decipher, I felt inadequate and out of place. Further, they spoke about their craft in a theoretical way that confused me and displayed an understanding of acting that far surpassed what I knew. They even laughed at and exploited my naïveté.

One evening they mentioned that they needed fresh

flowers for opening night. Norbert Davidson and a few of the older students asked if I would go with them to pick up flowers nearby. Flattered by their invitation, I agreed. We started walking toward the stores near the intersection of Gentilly and Elysian Fields. Taking what I thought was a shortcut, they turned in to the cemetery near the campus. I felt uncomfortable being in the cemetery at night but was afraid to express this fear to my cynical companions, who already thought I was unsophisticated. To my surprise, they walked up to a fresh grave site where flowers remained from a funeral earlier that day, took a floral arrangement, and began running back to campus. Aghast, I realized that the theft of graveside flowers had been their intention all along. I hurried back to the theater building, disappointed and angry at the deception and pained by the fact that I had been the butt of their humor. Furthermore, with my mother's death still weighing on my mind, I thought of those who mourned the unknown person buried in the grave and felt ashamed. Disappointed by the drama program and already uncertain about whether Dillard was right for me, I questioned whether I could fit in with the department's students and follow through on my plan to major in theater.

I found the theater faculty less charismatic than Miss Lillie. Elizabeth and Joe Greenhoe, a tall, lanky white couple who had trained at Yale, were instructor and assistant professor of Drama and Speech. Like many Dillard faculty of that era, this couple were civil rights activists from the North who came south to teach in Black colleges. They seemed out of place running the Theater Department, not because of their race but because they appeared out of touch with Black culture. Mr. Greenhoe, with his sad eyes, ungainly movements, and hesitant style, found it hard to convey his ideas to the rambunctious students. Unlike the faculty in other departments who, in the mode of the teachers I had at Wheatley, were inflexible and didactic in style, the Greenhoes were more Socratic, drawing us out with suggestions and questions. I had difficulty understanding this approach, particularly in acting class.

I knew nothing of Stanislavski or Method acting, in which one seeks to identify with a character's inner motivation. I was accustomed to memorizing lines and simply trying to deliver them in compelling ways. There was no particular method or theory to what I had been doing in high school. In one project in our acting class, Mr. Greenhoe directed us to become various assigned objects. How, I thought, does one become a chair or a cauliflower? This theoretical approach, as well as the methodology employed to free the actor of preconceived, predictable ways of being and responding, was more than I was prepared for. I squeaked by in the class, earning a B but learning very little. Since I had chosen Dillard so that I could become an actress, this was an immense blow.

In spite of my unhappiness with Mr. Greenhoe, I was spending a good deal of my time in Coss Hall, the Drama and Music Building. The motley gang of drama students gradually came to accept me. In spite of his role in the cemetery caper, the instigator, Norbert Davidson, befriended me and we were soon inseparable. Norbert was short, intense, and generally unkempt. He seemed to care nothing for the opinions of others, and I admired his independent spirit. Though from New Orleans, after graduating from Dillard he would earn an MFA from Stanford and become a professor of English. Most of all, he loved the arts and language and was different enough from the typical career-seeking Dillard student that I found him easy to be with. I had not begun to think about what I would ultimately do for a career; I still just wanted to learn, absorbing all that I could in preparation for a life of independence and courage doing whatever I saw fit to do. Norbert was laboring over a play he had conceived at Dillard, *El Hajj Malik,* about Malcolm X. It was, years later, hailed as a masterpiece and was produced in many venues around the world.

From a prominent and wealthy but dysfunctional family, Norbert had an extraordinary mind, a quick wit, and a sharp tongue. I admired his brilliance, command of language, and worldliness. His father, also named Norbert, was a well-known physician with whom his son did not get along. I was not certain of the origin of their disagreements, but it was clear that the younger Norbert was wealthier than other students and that this wealth had afforded him the opportunity to experience a good deal more of the world than most of us had. I had until then never known a person of my age who was as cultured and as sophisticated. Somewhat insecure, he must have enjoyed how I admired his knowledge and experience because he tolerated my friendship. While I was beginning to lose my passion for theater, Norbert was totally committed to it. He not only aspired to be a playwright but was an accomplished actor; his performance in the campus production of *Waiting for Godot* was especially memorable. I expected him to become a leading figure in American theater.

Norbert's fascination with Malcolm X revealed his strong interest in racial politics and the Civil Rights Movement. He had been involved in the types of acts of civil disobedience that were leading to desegregation of white establishments in the South. As a result of many discussions with him about our role in overturning segregation, I began to awaken to the Civil Rights Movement and consider for the first time what role I could play at such a pivotal moment in American history. Such thinking had been impossible while I was under my father's roof. Now I could begin to plan a path for myself that was not subject to parental approval. I thought about Antigone; the duty to become involved in passive resistance to unjust laws and practices was very much on my mind. Like other Black college students in the South at that time, I was made increasingly aware that change could not long be stayed.

We assembled frequently at Lawless Chapel to hear speeches by prominent religious and civic figures of the day, including civil rights activists who were leading that change. While there were no well-known firebrands on campus or organizations that pressed our involvement in protests in New Orleans, I knew we each had a duty to seek opportunities to become involved with the effort to overturn entrenched discrimination. Some of the Dillard faculty, through their academic work, revealed ways scholars could contribute expertise needed to overturn the disparate treatment of Blacks. Professors Daniel Thompson and Barbara Guillory were studying the slums of New Orleans and calling attention to the dire economic circumstances of Black families in housing projects. Groups such as the Community Relations Council of Greater New Orleans were bringing attention to the need for remedial action. Even as the work of these researchers and activists stoked an impatience with the status quo and encouraged activism, I resented any heavy-handed approach to shaping our thinking.

Now that I was questioning so much that I had taken for granted, my first-semester course in religion challenged my Black Baptist beliefs. Professor of Religion and Philosophy Roger Ward placed before us some fundamental questions about man's relationship to the world. Having never had to explore seriously the basis of my religious beliefs, I was shaken by these questions. As I considered possible reasons for and the results of man's reliance on a higher being and religious orthodoxies, I pondered the ways religion caused us to be patient, awaiting salvation. My introduction to philosophies that postulated different theories of human existence was pivotal. I was drawn to the reasoning of existentialists and their assertion that existence preceded essence. So different from my Baptist religious teachings, this idea struck me as a useful way to think about my life. I alone am responsible for my actions, I thought, and ultimately I will be no more than the sum of the actions I choose. I then turned this clarity of perspective about personal responsibility to considering inconsistencies in the behavior of religious leaders.

Remembering my father's behavior once he became a minister, I focused on inconsistencies between what religious leaders espoused and what they did. Where there were incongruities between the dictates of their faith and how they lived their lives, it seemed unlikely that they could transform the minds and hearts of others. More important, those ministers active in the civil rights struggle had a special duty to underscore that Blacks should not await the "sweet by-and-by" but take action to address oppression. I became even more enraged by my father's obsequiousness in the face of discrimination. Freedom would not come to Blacks simply because it was a God-given right; it would come only because enough people worked to bring about equality through concerted action. Such thinking would never have been tolerated among my family, but at Dillard I soon took it as a personal goal to find my own way to address racism and discrimination instead of relying on the patience that my father practiced.

I began to question the fairness of institutional practices in general and required chapel in particular. Religious worship, I argued, like other freedoms, should not be imposed. Because the college was affiliated with the Methodist Church, the Dillard administration was not sympathetic to that argument and naturally declined to eliminate the requirement. I decided, unilaterally, to boycott chapel. This was not a movement by any means but my effort to take a personal stand in regard to human freedom and equality. If there were Jews, Arabs, and Catholics on campus, how dare we force them to attend Protestant services? Of course, there were no Jews or Arabs. That hardly mattered to me. The principle mattered most, as would begin to be the case with many of my arguments—in college papers, in classroom debates, in the university newspaper, *Courtbouillon*. My rebellion lasted for the duration of my college days and well into my professional career. Challenging what I presumed to be unjust practices became my highest priority.

There was one moment, however, when I did not object to the role of the chapel on the campus. On November 22, three months after I had started college, news arrived that John F. Kennedy had been assassinated. Without hesitation, upon learning of his death, we all streamed into the chapel, seeking solace. I was embarrassed by the fact that an assassin had killed the president in my home state. My friends were already critical of Texas and now immediately voiced the belief that white racism in the state had killed the president. JFK's violent death brought back to me the memory of Mama's death, and for days I languished in renewed grief, watching the nation mourn and feeling again the complicated and debilitating helplessness I felt when I lost my mother. We all wept for Kennedy as if he were a parent taken suddenly from us, and, worse, we felt responsible for his death. We assumed that he was killed because he had supported the integration of schools in Little Rock and had come to the aid of Martin Luther King, Jr. I questioned what this might suggest about the prospect for civil rights and the direction of the country. We dedicated our 1964 yearbook, *Le Diable bleu,* to President and Mrs. John F. Kennedy: "In Tribute to Our Former President, John F. Kennedy."

We somehow got through the football season and Thanksgiving, when I was finally able to go home. There was little at home without Mama there. Still, it was good to have a break and to see family members again. But I said nothing to them of my activities or my courses. I didn't want them to think me pretentious, nor did I want to alarm them about the person I was becoming. Returning to Dillard after Thanksgiving, I decided that since I was not enjoying drama, I would finish the second semester and transfer. I would apply to Sarah Lawrence College, which had a strong arts program. By March, I had filed my application.

I had become president of the Straight Hall dormitory council but, aside from that and the Players Guild in Drama, anticipating that I would transfer, I kept my extracurricular involvement to a minimum. Campus social life was dominated by sororities and fraternities and New Orleans nightclubs, but I was not part of the sorority and party culture. And since my funds were very limited, I remained close to campus, studying and taking advantage of free events and activities. On rare occasions, friends invited me to join them off campus, but with so little money to spare, I was often pleased not to be asked. Yet I didn't feel at all unhappy with these limitations because I thought them to be temporary. By the spring semester, Sarah Lawrence had accepted me but offered no financial aid. I had to face the reality that I would be unable to transfer. Remaining at Dillard for three more years was an oppressive thought. I began to consider whether to drop out of college altogether.

That summer I returned to Houston and tried to decide what to do. If I didn't return to Dillard, where I had enough financial aid to pay for my education, I could see no way of completing college. Knowing that my siblings would not understand my dilemma, I withheld from them my apprehension about returning to Dillard. At summer's end, seeing no other choice, I decided to go back on the only terms I could imagine; I would change my major. I didn't confide this to Miss Lillie who, I knew, would be disappointed by my decision.

Returning to Dillard in the fall of 1964, I immersed my

self in literature and languages without a specific plan but as an effort to temporize in order to remain enrolled until I could decide on a definitive course. Lou LaBrant, like many northern scholars of the era, had moved to the South to play a role in the Civil Rights Movement by teaching Blacks. Her national leadership as president of the National Council of Teachers of English gave us access to scholarly talent equal to what students at more prestigious colleges enjoyed. Her exceedingly demanding and critical perspective on language usage helped improve my writing. I also enrolled in intermediate French with Yvonne Ryan, and intermediate Spanish with Ulysses Saucedo. Although I had never studied Spanish, Dr. Saucedo convinced me that since I had had French, I should be able to move directly into intermediate-level Spanish. In addition, I signed up for courses in history and math. I thought these classes would keep me busy and away from persistent thoughts of dropping out.

Dr. Saucedo turned out to be exactly the kind of teacher I had hoped to find. He was witty, fascinating, and deeply committed to language and literature. A cultured man of broad interests, he was developing a grammar on ancient Quechua, the indigenous language of Peru. He shared his research experiences with us and, a native speaker, he taught Spanish with infectious enthusiasm. Also a polyglot, he represented a way of life that I could imagine for myself. The field of language and literature as taught by Dr. Saucedo and Yvonne Ryan, opened my eyes to the importance of knowledge of different countries, cultures, and histories. Immersed in such study, I thought, I could easily cross racial and other societal boundaries. I considered becoming an interpreter or translator, or a teacher like Dr. Saucedo. His constant references to characters like Don Quixote intrigued me and made me want to go deeper into the authors and characters that made learning so enjoyable. I was relieved and happy to have found a satisfying alternative to theater. What could be better than spending my entire life in the world of literature, which had enchanted me when I was a child, taking me away from the difficulties of my circumstances? This choice would certainly mystify my family, who might expect more practical pursuits, so, once more, I kept my plans from them. Finally, I had found a way to remain at Dillard and finish college. Not wanting to disappoint all those who had helped me get there, I was happy with this solution.

Although I had abandoned theater, I continued to associate with many of the friends I had made in that department. Norbert Davidson and I had started to date, although I was frightened and intimidated by his intensity. I kept an emotional distance, a fact that he recognized, found annoying, and persistently criticized. As we spent less time together, a friend from Wheatley introduced me to a star player on the Bishop College basketball team. After the Bishop–Dillard game, we began writing to each other. Over the next months, this correspondence would grow into a long-distance courtship that would complicate my sophomore year at Dillard and my friendship with Norbert.

Chuck was from Rockford, Illinois, and, at twenty-seven years old, older than most students I knew. Articulate, suave, and self-assured, he already had a plan for his life that included getting married and settling into a middle-class routine. All too quickly, he cast me in a starring role in this rosy narrative and revealed his desire for us to marry. His ideal was not mine, especially because I had seen my mother trapped for so many years by a marriage that gave her so little independence. I knew that life with Chuck would leave me in a secondary role, paying obeisance to his ambition. Besides, I hardly knew him. My family, too, was skeptical. Erma Mae thought he was a bit of an operator; others expressed the view that, at nearly ten years my senior, he was simply too old for me. Family members were polite when he came home to Houston to visit but secretly hoped that I would come to my senses. In the end, I knew I wasn't ready to settle down. Once Dr. Saucedo, languages, and literature entered my plans, I was determined to study and travel. Chuck wanted a wife, not a scholar, so I gathered the courage to tell him that I could not marry him.

During this period, I became more involved in campus life, signing on to the newspaper, *Courtbouillon*. A courtbouillon is a kind of Cajun stew that incorporates many flavors and ingredients, especially anything on hand. Since I had to write papers for my classes and was becoming more proficient as a writer, it seemed easy to add articles for the newspaper to my responsibilities. I found that this work also fueled my interest in politics. More than anything, I marveled at how different my sophomore year was from the previous one. Now I loved Dillard and all of my classes. It frightened me to think I might have transferred. My academic performance improved, and I earned A's in all my courses except the first semester of world literature with Dr. LaBrant. In spite of his hopeful prediction that I would do well as a beginning student in intermediate Spanish, Dr. Saucedo felt I needed a stronger foundation in the language, so I asked the Worthing Foundation in Houston if I could use part of my scholarship to study in Mexico that summer. The executor of the fund approved the request, and I signed up for a month's study at the La Universidad Internacional in Saltillo.

That spring, just as the weather was turning warm, I was summoned to the university president's house. I immediately thought I was going to be upbraided or dismissed for the tone of an article I had written on boycotting chapel. Instead, arriving at the elegant manse, I learned astounding news: Dillard had selected me to attend Wellesley College for my junior year. Wellesley had designed the visiting junior program as a means of integrating the college by inviting ten juniors from different southern Black colleges to be resident students and take noncredit courses there for a year; Wellesley paid all expenses. President Dent told me what a rare opportunity this would be to study at one of the best colleges in the nation and that he was depending on me to represent Dillard well.

Honored to be selected, I finished the year aware that, within months, I would live in Mexico and then travel to Massachusetts. I recalled my disappointment at not being able to attend Sarah Lawrence. Yet, somehow, another way had emerged to achieve the goals I had set. I had come to Dillard to study theater and was now studying languages. The study of languages was leading to opportunities to travel and learn about other cultures. Had I transferred, these doors would not have opened for me. I had gained an invaluable lesson about how to handle disappointment, failure, and rejection: keep focusing on my goals, be flexible, and take advantage of alternative ways of achieving those goals. I hurried back to Houston to prepare for these new adventures. Finally, my yearning to learn about and live in a world beyond the segregation of Grapeland and Fifth Ward would become my way of being in the world.

11

Worlds Apart

FTER A FEW WEEKS OF REST IN HOUSTON, I BOARDED A Greyhound bus for Mexico. Recalling my train ride to Dillard, I was impressed that I was now brave enough to cross a boundary more daunting by far than my first train ride. To minimize the cost of travel, I had chosen a summer course at La Universidad Internacional in Saltillo, Coahuila, which was close to the Texas border. As the bus made its way through South Texas, across the Rio Grande, and through the mountains, it seemed barely able to maintain its perch on the highway. My fear of tumbling over the side into the canyons below resurrected my fear of heights from my days in Grapeland, but there may have been more to it than that. Perhaps it was a fear of what awaited me in the coming weeks. I did not permit myself to sleep on the long ride for fear I would dream of tumbling down into those fears.

I would be living with a Mexican family while studying at the university, and I sensed that the experience in such a different environment could be challenging given my limited Spanish language skills.

Arriving in Saltillo, I took a taxi to Apartado 293, where I was delighted to find a modest yet appealing little residence. The owner of the house, an elderly woman, greeted me and showed me my room, which was in the rear of the house and off the courtyard, with its blue and white patterned tiles and potted plants. The room was unpretentious but comfortable; the handsome furnishings, so different from what I was accustomed to, looked massive in the small space. The colors in the house, cheerful and friendly, suggested an open and lively culture.

The institute, while orderly and efficient in getting all the new students settled into classes, was another matter. Being so near the U.S. border, it was filled with southern Americans who traveled to Mexico to study Spanish and vacation. In the course of our three weeks of intensive study, we had four courses on grammar, conversation, and vocabulary, which alternated with outings into town and, on weekends, to other sites, such as Mexico City. Though I was very motivated to learn Spanish, I found the environment challenging. Some of the participants reacted negatively to having a Black student in their classes, and they would shout out insults if I spoke in class. One day, after I answered a question, one of them shouted, "The South shall rise again!" Given what had happened in the South so recently, with the suppression of the Southern Christian Leadership Conference's Birmingham campaign, I was uncertain whether to expect mischief or even violence from my fellow students in Saltillo. Being the only Black in the program, I decided that the best course was to keep a low profile, going to class and returning to my residence immediately afterward. I had imagined that being in a foreign environment could be a challenge, but I had not considered that racial incidents from the United States would follow me there. It was an important lesson.

Returning to Houston in late July, I began preparing for the next adventure, Wellesley College. Family members must have been concerned about my peregrinations but said nothing to discourage me from leaving for another strange new destination. Yet no one except my brothers while in military service and my basketball playing Prairie View brother, Clarence, had traveled extensively. Certainly none of my sisters had ventured so far from home. I don't know if my father realized what these decisions meant for my future, but he showed no interest in my plans and made no effort to prevent my going so far away. So, with no opposition, a few weeks later, I took my first airplane trip, bound for Boston.

Wellesley College is located in a small town about fifteen miles from Boston. Students traveled easily between Wellesley and Boston via commuter rail. Nestled in this small town, the college's five hundred acres constituted a stately campus, with a tower housing a carillon that was played between classes and on special occasions. Beyond the setting overlooking a lake and the landscape design, which incorporated an unusual variety of grasses and trees, the tuneful carillon gave the campus an added measure of importance. While not as beautiful as Dillard, it was attractive.

As guest juniors, the students arriving from Black colleges had a brief orientation, after which each of us was assigned to a different dormitory, limiting our ability to establish close friendships with one another. White Wellesley students had been chosen to help us get settled. Assigned to Stone Hall, I was placed on the hallway of an unambiguously congenial group of juniors who immediately came to my aid as I tried to adjust to this new environment where, much as in Saltillo, I felt out of place. My brief sojourn in Saltillo had been my first experience in a racially integrated learning and living environment. My new hall mates were friendly, but as I gradually came to understand the history associated with this preeminent Seven Sisters campus, I thought that Wellesley students might be too rich and elitist to befriend a person of my background. It was obvious that the other students on the hallway came from families of significant stature and means. Not knowing what this disparity in circumstances would mean, I was watchful for evidence of their scorn. The girls spoke excitedly of all the things I would be able to do during my year at Wellesley: travel, go into Boston to mixers at Harvard and MIT, ski, and so on. I knew that I would have difficulty managing such activities within my meager budget.

I had arrived in Massachusetts without proper clothing for the climate. It was already cooler than I had anticipated and, with winter coming soon, some encouraged me to go to a clothing exchange to find warmer clothing and a coat. A local host family, the Browns, volunteered to offer me off-campus hospitality and assistance. Louise Brown, an Alabaman, was the friendliest and kindest adult white person I had met; she and her husband helped me solve my initial problems in understanding where to go for different needs and included me in their family gatherings. With a large, active family and a southern background, they were an ideal host family for me. Finding a transplanted southerner, who understood my background and whom I enjoyed more than the liberal northerners I met, was one of many surprises in my first encounter with the North. At the time, we tended to equate northerners with friendliness, concern, and solidarity with oppressed southern Blacks, and white southerners as uncompromisingly racist. Finding Mrs. Brown, with her thick southern accent, to be the antithesis of a racist shamed me into recognizing my responsibility to avoid relying on the same kinds of stereotypes that had so long imprisoned me and my family. The Browns helped me adjust to Wellesley without any apparent thought that I was less deserving than their own children.

Finances continued to weigh on my mind as I searched for appropriate winter clothing and shoes. My first letter home from Box 86, Stone Hall, on September 16, 1965, shows my preoccupation. Once again, I turned to Wilford, on whom I relied for all my needs. He never disappointed me.

Dear Wilford,

Well, my third day here and I'm just beginning to get the hang of things. I went to Boston today and looked for a warm coat. I also rode the subway for the first time, saw Boston Common, and had my first hot pastrami in a delicatessen.

It's just September and it's 45 degrees in the mornings. I freeze every night with 3 blankets on my bed.

*I hate to think about what it'll be like when winter
really comes. Right now, I hear the radiator finally
coming on.*

*They're doing everything possible to make the guest
juniors comfortable. There are 10 of us altogether but
I seldom see the others because we all live in different
dormitories. This is such a huge campus that I have
been to only 4 buildings since I've been here.*

*Most students bank at a bank not far from here—
Wellesley National bank [sic] and I gather there is a
bit of difficulty cashing checks if you don't have a bank
account. Most of the students write checks instead of
using cash.*

Tomorrow I have to get over and buy some books.

*Send the money in a money order so that I'll [sic]
no problems with a check.*

I'll write when I get time.

Love to everybody.
Ruth

I eventually found a job cleaning houses, and the additional money, along with small amounts from home, helped
me afford a coat and pay for an occasional trip to HoJo's
(Howard Johnson's restaurant) for fried clams. I thought
about the fact that I was now cleaning houses as my mother
had done under very different circumstances. Somehow, the
fact that I was working in this way reassured me that I was
not losing touch with my background, and I promised myself
never to become so attached to this new life that I lost my

appreciation for the history, culture, and people that had shaped me.

Gradually, I began to feel more at ease with the high teas and other stuffy Wellesley traditions. Over the course of the year, I grew close to one girl, Lisa, and visited her large family on their Connecticut farm. I visited other hall mates at their homes in Philadelphia and, during my Fulbright year, Switzerland. Lisa took me on my first skiing trip, to Stowe, Vermont, and there were numerous other adventures in Boston and Cambridge over the course of the year.

Most important to me were the courses I took. My classes were far more challenging than any I had ever had. As a junior, I was expected to follow the course of study of a French major when, in fact, I had had only one year of college French at Dillard. I enrolled in English 107 (Interpretation of Man in Western Literature), French 201 (French Literature Through the Ages), and French 224 (Speech), as well as Spanish 204 (The Novel and Essay in Spanish Literature). Because of my stint in Mexico, my Spanish was better than my French. To my horror, French classes at Wellesley were taught in French. Although we had practiced conversational French at Dillard, I had never heard a native speaker and had never held a full conversation in French. I was distraught that I could not understand anything the professor was saying, and after a month of feeling lost and missing oral assignments, I went to ask him if I might drop the course. He encouraged me to continue, and with what I took to be indifference, declared "Ne vous inquiétez pas! Ayez patience!" Don't worry? Just be patient? I was drowning.

Not having a choice, I went to class every day, studied for hours, and played French tapes in the language laboratory. To my surprise, one day several weeks later, I discovered that I was beginning to understand spoken French. That moment of recognition was one of the most powerful in my entire experience as a student. Catching up with the class and understanding French had seemed impossible to me, and now with time and effort I was able to capture most of what my professor was saying! Not only that, I was studying alongside white students from very privileged educational backgrounds. To some degree, I must have questioned whether my Fifth Ward education, my preparation at Dillard, and my limited experience would measure up to the challenge of one of the best colleges in the country, and in that instant of recognition and empowerment, I realized that I needed never to doubt myself again.

In the second semester, I took three more French courses and a Classical Philosophy course. One day we were discussing justice, and the example of South African apartheid came up. The class members were arguing the importance of eliminating this racist policy when a girl from South Africa spoke up, defending it. For a moment, people reacted with disbelief. Speaking softly, she concluded her remark by saying, "It's our country, too." Initially offended by her defense of this violation of human rights, I began to recognize that her presence had changed the tenor of our runaway condemnation of all white South Africans. If she had not been present, the perspective of white South Africans would have been entirely absent from our heated debate. I saw that just hearing different perspectives inevitably changed and broadened my understanding of any subject. I remembered the many times I had wanted to absent myself when the class debate turned to civil rights or the condition of Blacks in the United States. Being the lone Black student had made me feel uncomfortable, and I had often elected to remain silent. Yet this student was willing to be the lone spokesperson for white South Africans, and however misguided her reasoning in justifying apartheid, I admired her willingness to speak out. I realized I should do no less.

My year in Massachusetts had been transformative in many ways. After Mexico, I learned once again that I could tolerate and benefit from being in a different racial and cultural environment. My doubt about my intellectual ability receded as I grew to understand that I could handle the challenging work of an elite college. I formed friendships with young women from vastly different backgrounds and found comfort in finally escaping the racial segregation of the previous nineteen years of my life. Finally, a picture of what my future might become came into focus. Even so, I would not have anticipated that I would one day be selected to lead a college like Wellesley. Today I know that, without my experience as a Wellesley student, I might never have become president of Smith College. Not being able to attend Sarah Lawrence, though a disappointment at the time, led me to an opportunity that placed me on the path to three college presidencies.

As the year neared an end, my friends suggested that I go to France for the summer. Some had been on the Experiment in International Living, a program that sponsored American students who would spend time in a French family's home and tour a part of the country afterward. I applied and managed to secure a scholarship. With the news that I would be able to go to France in the summer, I began to wonder whether returning to Dillard for my senior year was a good idea. I knew that I would not have comparable French courses there. I went to see Dean Frisch about transferring to Wellesley. The college was adamant: transferring was out of the question. The agreement with the Black colleges was that visiting juniors would not be permitted to transfer to Wellesley.

I left in June for France. Led by Jane Simon, an experienced group leader, our experimenters group went first to Paris and a few days later traveled by train to our host site, Metz, in Alsace-Lorraine. Dressed in my favorite outfit for the ride on the rapide, I was concerned about making a good impression when I met my French host family at the Metz station. My navy dress was made of a linen-like synthetic with white trim around the neck and sleeves that spilled down the sides and encircled the dress just below the waistline. Three large white buttons were arrayed across the front just above the horizontal band. Arriving in Metz on June 30, the twelve experimenters were directed to the Salon Verlaine du Buffet, where we had a brief reception and met our host families. Madame Andre Weber, the local organizer, spoke to us, and we were photographed for the local newspaper, *Le Républicain lorrain*. The pride and excitement at our arrival was reflected in an effusive description on page 4 of the July 1, 1965, edition of the paper.

The description captured the spirit of our reception throughout our time in Metz. My host family had two daughters, one of whom was to be my companion. Brigitte, tall and somewhat shy, was delightful, and I liked her immediately. Her family's apartment was a handsome, comfortable middle-class residence. I did not know much about the family's background and was afraid to ask, thinking that it would be impolite. Brigitte's mother was a housewife, and her father, small in stature, was somewhat dictatorial; Madame would scurry to comply with his instructions at the slightest rise in his voice. I laughed at how he was so much like my father in Texas. Male dominance did not seem to have any problem crossing frontiers! The two girls in the family were not intimidated by their father's gruffness and often poked fun at him, to his delight. They had planned activities for me in Metz, and we traveled to the Saar region, and to Nancy. They loved to see me react to their customs and took care to explain things that I might not understand. Brigitte, a college student, spoke rapidly but, while it was at times difficult to follow her, after Wellesley, I found conversing with her to be entirely manageable.

The object of curiosity as the only Black student in my group, I was amazed to be received so well by both my host family and my fellow experimenters. At home, I was treated like one of the daughters in the family; in the larger group, I was just another experimenter. When the time came to leave Metz for the second part of the trip, I realized I would miss this wonderful family, so much like my own close family far away in Texas.

I was also worried about my inadequate bicycling skills, because we were headed south for our "circuit touristique de camping dans le sud de la France," our bicycle tour of southern France. My very recent efforts to learn to ride a bicycle had been so brief that I feared I would make a fool of myself. The first day on the road was difficult and painful but, fortunately, we did not start out ambitiously. We took the train south to Avignon, where we had arranged to collect our bicycles. We were to ride to a new town each day, camp overnight, and move on to another town the next day. In August, the countryside was hot and the sun punishing, but we were able to rest at noon and whenever we came to a town where we had the excuse to stop and sightsee. We cycled through Arles, Pont du Gard, Les Baux-de-Provence, Aigues-Mortes, and Saintes-Maries-de-la-Mer. I marveled at the Roman ruins and aqueducts; the beautiful vineyards, from which we sampled grapes; the marshes of Camargue; and the steep cliffs of Les Baux.

I continued to write Wilford about my adventures, but I still did not feel comfortable telling other family members about my time so far from home. I did not know how to convey what I was experiencing to my family back in Houston or to my friends at Dillard. How could I speak of the beautiful train ride to the south of France or the ride along the Camargue on horseback without an air of self-importance? I was at once embarrassed to be able to enjoy these experiences when they could not and concerned that this new life would create a barrier between me and them. That feeling has remained as, even today, my life is immensely different from those of most of my siblings.

Back home, my family was mired in the limited opportunities available to them. I did not want to lose sight of that reality, to which I also belonged. I also feared losing my identity. I pondered how I would recognize whether I had adopted the attitude of entitlement that I could see in my new acquaintances' behavior; that would surely alienate me from my previous life and my family. Most of all, I didn't want to covet this new life and redefine myself to fit its demands. Still, it hardly seemed possible that, having lived in total segregation all of my life, I would in one year's time live in Mexico, study at an elite women's college on my first trip to the North, and travel to France to live with a French family and bicycle through Provence. The Fifth Ward was receding rapidly and my perspective on life was changing.

The experiences of that remarkable year shaped my career in ways that I could never have anticipated. The challenging academics at Wellesley prepared me to apply for the Fulbright and Danforth Fellowships that I won in my senior year. My greater fluency in French enabled me to study at the Université de Lyon as a Fulbrighter and work as an interpreter for the State Department when I returned to the United States. After completing graduate school at Harvard and working for a time as a professor and administrator, I became president of Smith College, the nation's largest women's college. I cannot be certain that any of these milestones would have been possible without that year stretching from Mexico to Wellesley to France.

12

Commencement

FTER AN EXHAUSTING SIX WEEKS IN FRANCE, I RETURNED to Texas for a brief rest and reintroduction to Fifth Ward and my family before going back to Dillard for my senior year. I made the rounds of my sisters' and brothers' homes, seeing how my nieces and nephews had grown and enjoying southern food again. The more I experienced outside of my family's frame of reference, the less I spoke about my adventures to my family. Among them, I wanted to be Ruth Jean (I had long ago dropped the pretentious "e"s), fitting into the family as I always had. I knew that my travels seemed odd to my sisters and brothers. They all wanted to be in Houston near the rest of the family and couldn't understand my need for the outside world.

I was uncertain how I would feel about returning to Dillard, a campus that I had outgrown. Would I show my impatience with narrow perspectives, my disdain for rigid administrative policies, my concern about the lack of cultural diversity? Knowing that the year would be busy and intense as I decided what to do upon graduating helped me relax and understand that I didn't need to try to change Dillard. It had stood for a long time, successfully helping Black students transform their prospects for successful lives. While it could not compete with Wellesley's academic strength, it was perhaps doing something more important: addressing the economic and social disparities that Black communities continued to suffer because of racism. Hadn't it enabled such a transformation in my life?

As I thought about my next steps, the one thing that seemed clear was that I would be unlikely to return to Houston. I felt more removed from Daddy than ever, in turn polite but distant when I was in his presence. I could not tell him that my courses and experiences had made me even more critical of his religious calling and harsh treatment of his wife and children. Just as important in the distance between us was his unchanged belief in the inferior role of women. I had come to see my life in very different terms.

I had no feminist courses or any overt teaching about the role of women, but I had come to understand that my father and mother had reared me to play a submissive and secondary role. Women prepared food, served men, and ate last. Women obeyed their husbands. Women did not participate in serious discussions with men. Women did not wear pants. Women did not lead. Women could not be preachers. Women should not talk back. I knew that I could never have that life. My goal was to be independent enough that I would never have to suffer mistreatment, abuse, or denigration.

In my first two years at Dillard, the ideal of Black women being subservient to and secondary to Black men still held sway. We were to act like ladies and to let the boys be in charge. Girls could lead if there was no boy available for that role. But our duty was to bolster the self-confidence and psyches of the men who, after all, were the prime targets of white fear and loathing. It was our duty to restore their dignity, and that could be done only by subjecting ourselves to their indignities. I rejected this reasoning, hoping that mutual respect was a better solution than the oppression of Black girls and women. Wellesley had helped remove my reticence about speaking out against such treatment. But not to my father.

It had not occurred to me before my year at Wellesley that women could lead; the most powerful women I had met were teachers. All my principals had been men. When I first saw Margaret Clapp, president of Wellesley, during an afternoon tea at Stone Hall, it became clearer to me that the subservience of women was manifestly less a function of women's limitations and more a function of men's willful efforts to retain their own privileges. Was not the same dynamic operating when white people imposed subservience on Blacks? Wellesley was full of women leading, making decisions, designing programs, overseeing budgets. Though I didn't see her as a particularly charismatic person, the simple fact that Margaret Clapp was the president of the college made an impact on me. I neither got to know her well nor saw a lot of her during my year there. It was enough to know that the campus, its faculty and students, had an accomplished woman as president. From that moment on my conviction grew that I should not accept the ludicrous proposition that women were predisposed to fail at challenging assignments. I returned to Dillard unwilling to hold back, to do just enough to be successful but not enough to be first.

My first days back were awkward, confirming my fears. Seeing this small campus of nine hundred students, I remembered France and Boston and all the places I had been. Dillard no longer seemed the grand place it had been before. The students chattered about local matters when I wanted to discuss national and international affairs. They were interested in the next social or who was seeing whom, and I wanted to find a discussion group to share ideas. Luckily, I was able to share a room with Gemma Douglas, a friend from Birmingham, Alabama, who was thoughtful, mature, and interested in the world outside Dillard. Gemma was raised by her grandmother, who was a teacher and one of the most inspiring women I had met. Though her grandmother was close in age to my own parents, she was worldly, accomplished, and open-minded, qualities she imparted to Gemma. With her freckles, reddish complexion, and impish humor, Gemma was fun to be around. Finally, I had a roommate with whom I had something in common.

Continuing with French and Spanish, I found the Dillard courses interesting but too easy. I tried to remain engaged by seeking additional work. Fortunately, I had a full course on existentialism, a subject that I continued to find engrossing. Reading Nietzsche, Sartre, Kierkegaard, I grew more convinced that I should focus on my actions. Thunderstruck by Jean-Paul Sartre, I read everything by him that I could find and promised myself eventually to read his works in the original French. I tried to apply Sartre's empowering philosophy to my own life. It was what I needed to resolve the conflict and guilt I felt about leaving my familial culture behind. Sartre wrote of an authentic life, shaped by one's own hands. The image of dirty hands, "les mains sales," in his play of that name, was an apt metaphor for what I thought my life should be. In any case, the life I would live would be my own, no matter what. I could freely claim it as such and embrace my responsibility and freedom to act. And act I did.

That semester I threw myself not only into my courses but also into numerous activities. I became editor of the campus newspaper, *Courtbouillion,* and I recruited my best friends to work with me. Our articles reflected our opinions on and critiques of Dillard. We editorialized about the apathy of the student body, the quality of discourse on campus, and the dominance of Greek hazing. My sarcastic tone is evident in a December 1966 editorial on hazing entitled "It's Greek to Me."

My righteous indignation ascended to a new level. If there was a sacred cow, I wanted to poke it. It was not that I was angry, but I had, after all, become a crusader, taking seriously my duty to act. With such an attitude, I did not endear myself to fellow students who continued to think me, if not odd, a memorable character. But I was no longer playing a role; I was searching for a way to be relevant and engaged at a moment when so many were on picket lines protesting injustices. After I had met so many new people in Mexico, Massachusetts, and France, my interests lay in what contribution I could make to the world. Becoming an outspoken academic seemed to hold promise. By October, with deadlines for fellowships and graduate school admissions ahead, I began applying with a vengeance. Completing applications for Yale, Harvard, and Berkeley, and, later, Case Western as a backup, I waited for decisions. My first choice was Yale, which at the time had the best graduate program in French. At the same time, I applied for independent fellowships: from the Fulbright Program as well as Woodrow Wilson and Danforth Fellowships.

Gemma was dating Ralph Edwards, a member of the class of '68. He was different from most of the boys on campus, smart, serious, and sensitive. Gemma and I were looking for boys who had more to offer than a glib line and limited ambitions, and Ralph stood out as someone who could go places. After his sophomore year at Dillard, Ralph had transferred to Tulane University, where he thought he could fit in better, perhaps, as a bit of an egghead. He and Gemma had grown closer in my year at Wellesley and were devoted to each other. One day they convinced me to go on a date with Ralph's Tulane University roommate, Norbert Simmons. I could hardly believe there was another Black man named Norbert, let alone one I should date, but I agreed.

Norbert was from New Orleans and one of the first Blacks to integrate Tulane. For those at Dillard, Tulane was like Harvard, so I could not help but be impressed that someone had integrated such a forbidding place. Ralph spoke about the challenges of being a Black student there and, with my experiences at Saltillo and Wellesley, I understood how lonely and difficult that could be. My first impression of Norbert was that he was trying too hard. Too hard to be witty. Too hard to be liked. Too hard to be polished. Too hard to be interested. I was puzzled that he and Ralph were friends because Ralph seemed far more serious. Nevertheless, we had a date. He took me to a New Orleans nightclub where we sat and had drinks. He was polite and extremely courteous, almost courtly. Everything about him was proper: his speech, his stiff smile, his clothing, his haircut. He drove a small Corvair with a sticker on the dashboard that said "Jackie." I asked him about it and learned later that although he suggested that this was the name of a previous girlfriend, the sticker had been on the car when he purchased it. I thought the invention odd and unwarranted since we didn't know each other well.

He had been raised by his aunt and uncle, Ora and Alonzo Brooks, who had adopted him when he was a young child. Alonzo had other children from a previous marriage but no children with Ora. Norbert was the child Ora had always wanted, and she was completely devoted to him. Alonzo was a quirky, imperious man who had been a chauffeur for a wealthy uptown New Orleans family. He always boasted that he had once driven Haile Selassie. Old fashioned to a fault, he was also quite dictatorial. He wanted Norbert to be a doctor, and nothing less would do. It was already clear that Norbert's heart and ability did not lie in that direction, but he didn't dare tell his family. After a few dates, he took me to meet Alonzo and Ora in their middle-class Pontchartrain Park home. I felt immediately at home with the old-fashioned couple.

Norbert became more and more the center of my attention as the year advanced. Although we spent a good deal of time together, I still didn't think I knew him. He seemed to orchestrate what he wanted me to know, and I was already beginning to doubt the accuracy of some of what he told me. Although he had introduced us, Ralph seemed cool to the idea of my becoming close to Norbert. I did not press him for the reasons. What was evident was that both Norbert and I had aspirations that placed us in a different category from most of our peers. We talked about graduate and professional school, about what life might be like elsewhere, about changes under way in the country, and how we could play a role in improving society. I shared with him my life at Wellesley and my travels around France without any fear that he would think them pretentious. However, our relationship remained platonic. Busy with my plans for graduate school, I accepted this status with some relief.

In my French major, classes with Yvonne Ryan continued to be very satisfying, even if they were less demanding than I would have wished. Miss Ryan came to us by way of Tulane. Blacks tended to be distrustful of southern accents at that time; they spelled racial hatred for many. Decidedly a white southerner with a drawl that hampered her French accent, Miss Ryan nevertheless was very open-minded and devoted to her Dillard students. She invited us to her home and treated us as peers. Although her spoken facility in French was not up to the native ability of professors at Wellesley, she was an excellent teacher of literature. As I began to think of graduate schools, she guided me toward the right universities and provided an example of what I could expect if I became a professor of French. So many of my Dillard professors were white like Miss Ryan: Lou LaBrant, Professor of English and Chair of Humanities; Dr. Saucedo, my Spanish professor; the Greenhoes in Drama, and Professor Ward in Philosophy. I found it ironic that many of my mentors at my Black college were white.

In the spring semester, as Mardi Gras approached, I decided to invite Lisa, my best friend and Stone Hall classmate from Wellesley, to visit. She and her family had been so good to me, inviting me to their Connecticut farm and making me feel welcome, and I wanted to show her a good time in New Orleans. I alerted my friends including Norbert that Lisa was coming and made arrangements for us all to take her to a Mardi Gras parade. After Lisa arrived, I tried to reach Norbert, but he did not return my calls. After having so excitedly told Lisa about my boyfriend and seeing how she wanted to meet him, I was embarrassed that Norbert was mysteriously unavailable.

Proceeding with our plans to enjoy the parade without him, Ralph stepped in to drive us. Afterward, while returning to campus, we saw Norbert pulling onto Gentilly Boulevard with a girl in his car. Ralph pulled up alongside his car to make certain Norbert was aware that we had seen him. We learned that he had a girlfriend visiting from out of town. Although he and I had not declared a commitment to each other, my trust in him was shaken. I was to revisit this incident many times in the coming years as Norbert and I married and started a family. He continued his secretive ways, and the distrust I felt became too difficult to overcome; we dissolved our marriage after ten mostly happy years and two wonderful children.

As the end of the school year neared, I had a number of issues to resolve with Dillard. The first was that they did not

know how to treat my ungraded year at Wellesley. I was mak-·
ing all A's in my final year, but my lackluster performance in
my freshman year, with a B plus average, and the absence of
grades in my junior year meant that I would not be graduating with honors. In addition, my boycotting of chapel during
freshman year remained a serious problem for the university
and, because of it, I might not graduate at all. I sent a letter
to my family informing them of this issue. My greatest concern was that I might not be able to go to graduate school or
accept any fellowship I might receive.

Then, good news began to trickle in. I was awarded a
Fulbright to study in France and a Danforth Fellowship to
study anywhere I wished in the United States. Rejected by
Yale, I was admitted to Harvard.

The rejection by Yale was the first I had had in a while, and
it shook my confidence. I wondered whether it was more a
matter of their department concluding that someone from a
Black college could not do the level of work required at Yale.
The attitude of elite colleges toward students who study at
Black colleges was then and continues to be a personal disappointment. Perhaps that is what led me to try over the entirety
of my career to expose and overturn such elitist attitudes. But,
in the end, going to Harvard turned out to be empowering and
a great advantage in achieving my ambitious goals.

With the news of my fellowships and Harvard admission,
Dillard relented. Recognizing that if I did not graduate they
would be unable to announce that a Dillard student had won
both a Danforth and a Fulbright Fellowship and would be
going to Harvard, they dropped the issue of my nonatten-

dance at chapel. They also decided to allow me to graduate summa cum laude in spite of the missing junior grades.

I began planning to spend the next year abroad. Securing permission from the Danforth Foundation to hold my fellowship until I returned from France, I decided to pursue a research project on the writer Marcel Proust at the Université de Lyon. What could be better than a glorious year reading Proust. I couldn't believe my good fortune to be able to delve into his dense prose and explore deeply the experience of recapturing lost time. The famous epiphany that most associate with Proust's *À la Recherche du temps perdu,* in which a character's memories of the past come rushing back to him, resonated with my efforts to recall my experiences "up home." Was there something in Proust's methodology that could help me reconcile the disjunction that I was feeling? I was now a part of such different worlds: one was educated, worldly, and socially active; the other was isolated, unsophisticated, and imprisoned in the dictates of others. Yet I was constantly trying to return to the place of my childhood, which had imparted values I somehow knew I would need in my life.

To study and reflect under the mentorship of Marcel Proust, I would need a place to reside. I wrote to my French family in Metz and asked if they might know someone in Lyon from whom I could rent a room. They recommended a Madame Kraft, and I quickly secured a room in her home. Graduation from Dillard itself seemed insignificant next to what lay beyond.

Norbert, a junior at Tulane, informed me that he had also applied for study abroad and that he would be going to the

University of Warwick in England during the fall semester. In spite of my misgivings about his secrecy, we made a pact to see each other during our time away and quickly began coordinating our next year's calendars. I was relieved that someone I knew would be relatively close by, visiting when time allowed.

Commencement finally arrived. Some of my family and the Lillies were planning on attending, and I suspected that none of them realized how well I had actually done the previous four years. I had avoided telling anyone about my grades. My father made no comment about graduation, nor did he try to attend, but four of my sisters and brothers—Wilford, Elbert, Nora, and Atherine—came. The drive from Houston was long and on two-lane roads much of the way, and because they had to get back to their jobs, they drove straight through and returned home without spending the night. I could not believe they took the time to come to see me graduate. Through all the years following my mother's death, these four had done everything possible to assure that I grew up as Mama would have wished. They fed me, supported my efforts (even when they might not have understood them), cheered me on, and watched over me just as she knew they would when we moved to Houston. I realized that she had finally let go because of her confidence that they would not abandon the younger children. And they had not. I was deeply moved and proud to be part of such a close family.

It was also fitting that the Lillies came. They had supported me throughout my years at Dillard. When I told friends that my high school teacher and her family were coming to graduation, they were mystified. "Are they relatives?"

they asked. "No," I answered, "but they are like family to me." That was to remain the case well beyond my college years.

The day of graduation we all lined up on the esplanade of oaks for the final ceremony of our Dillard days. I could not help but think back to the doubts I'd had when I first arrived there. As I reflected on the previous four years, I marveled at the transformation I had undergone. The pain of my mother's death had not disappeared, but it had receded enough for me to move on with my life. The Worthing and Danforth Scholarships had opened a series of doors for me. In the courses and struggles on the campus, I had found myself not the person I had created in high school, who was full of affectation and pretension, but one who grew up and accepted the responsibility to be independent and constructive. In the four years of liberal arts courses, I found a reservoir of inspiration and insight into the question of what my life could be. It could be an ongoing quest for deep understanding of who I am. It could be a role in a historic moment of societal transformation. Although I did not have the exact formula for the self-improvement I sought, I recognized that I was now better equipped to face the process. Mama was, of course, on my mind, as she was at any major occasion or moment of transition. I longed again to see her and to have her know what had become of me. I no longer believed that she was looking down on me in a literal sense; but I certainly felt that, if I were measuring whether I had followed her admonitions and her moral guidance, I could give myself at least a B.

As we marched down the esplanade to our seats on the lawn in front of Kearney Hall, I could see my sisters and brothers and the Lillies. Soon, I heard President Dent talking about me—about my year at Wellesley and about my having won the Fulbright and Danforth Fellowships as well as admission to Harvard. I was embarrassed but happy to have him celebrate my accomplishments in front of my family and the Lillies. I thought that nothing in the future could exceed my pride and happiness on that glorious day.

EPILOGUE

STUDENTS OFTEN ASK ME HOW I CAME THROUGH THE DIFFICULT periods of my life without looking back in anger. I am always startled by this question. Any life is, after all, the sum of a variety of contingencies leavened by whatever order and understanding we are able to bring to them. I do not regard the circumstances of my childhood as more difficult or more glorious than another's. What ultimately matters in any life is whether, at every point, we are sufficiently attentive to what has been lost and gained, and whether that knowledge usefully informs us about how to live out the rest of our lives. The disappointment of my father refusing to help me go to college, my inability to continue my plans to study acting, the refusal of Sarah Lawrence and Yale to help me attend—all forced me to confront the reality that one path foreclosed is an invitation to consider other opportunities that could be equally, and, possibly even more, satisfying and beneficial. I was able to move on, always hopeful about what I might learn and how I might grow. And so, I answer the students' questions by saying that I have lived my life by trying to learn as much as possible from everything, good and bad, placed on my path. Every loss. Every gain. Every hurt. Every triumph.

Without the extraordinary people I have encountered in every decade of my life, I could not have been as well prepared to understand how to travel the road from Grapeland to the heights of American higher education. Through them— the gifted teachers, my family, and the many others who mentored or chided me—I could not have fully benefited from the many opportunities I have encountered. Caring people placed me on the path to the presidencies of Smith, Brown, and then, back home, Prairie View, and education helped me overcome the way my life might have been scripted by the legacy of discrimination. Whatever one says about the troubles of public schools, for a child born into poverty, a public school teacher can be, and often is, the only thing keeping despair at bay. Forgotten by hope and denied opportunity, how can such a child learn to focus on what the future could bring? Had it not been for my teachers showing me that barriers to learning could be scaled, I might have given up. Had it not been for the books that taught me there was more to reality than what I could see and touch, I might have joined the many youth who never come to know achievement. Had it not been for the exhilaration I felt about school, I might never have thought my life could forever be filled with wondrous adventures and satisfying accomplishments.

I am not the one to judge whether I have made the most of the opportunities afforded me by a combination of misfortune, hard work, and support from loved ones and strangers. I do know that to stand where I am today, looking back on my childhood, I find it difficult to imagine that I could have gone from the crossroads of Grapeland, Texas, to the presidencies of Smith College, Brown University, and Prairie View A&M without some miraculous intervention that could turn crude cotton sacks into silk.

By the grace of my grandparents Richard and Emma, my parents, Fannie and Ike, and all my brothers and sisters, I came to believe that the human spirit could overcome extraordinary trials. Richard and Emma Campbell planted the seeds of our survival when they bought and settled sixty acres of farmland west of Grapeland near the Trinity River. Fannie and Ike Stubblefield, notwithstanding all that came between them and the overwhelming odds they faced, stayed together to rear twelve children and provide for their basic needs. Along the way Fannie instilled in us the need to respect others as well as ourselves, to be upright and hardworking, and to appreciate and preserve familial bonds. I was impatient with these teachings when I was young but, with age and experience, I came to see how hard it must have been for my grandparents and parents. When I had children of my own, I marveled at what the generations before me were able to accomplish with so little education, so few resources, and so little freedom.

The childhood I had was typical of many of my era and place. Others may have lived these events better than I, but I think few could have lived them with more seriousness of purpose and gratitude. When my mother died, I awoke to the fact that, whether we desire it or not, everything we experience matters and can change the direction of our lives. That most devastating moment when she took her leave impelled me in a direction that led to all I have become and all I have accomplished. That, with my father's disinterest in my ambition, gave me the freedom to leave home in a determined search for a life of independence, dignity, and purpose. Every circumstance, including the racism that shaped my parents' lives and the segregated world that threatened to stunt my achievement, held promise.

At every commencement, I look out over the assembled students and consider the kinds of events, choices, and limitations that might await them. I pray that they will discover, in time, that they can rely on their learning to help them face every opportunity and every crisis in a productive way. I hope they can go beyond any constraints others have set for them and work tirelessly to become the person they dream of being. Most of all, I am grateful if they have learned the value of being open to ways that the differences among people they meet can make them stronger and more adaptable to the change they will encounter.

I hope that they have learned this, in part, by observing me as I carry out my duties as their president. For, thanks to the opportunities granted me to learn, I am not the person I was supposed to be. Rather, I am the person that I dreamed of becoming.

ABOUT THE AUTHOR

RUTH J. SIMMONS is the president of Prairie View A&M University, Texas's oldest HBCU, as well as the former president of Brown University and Smith College and former vice provost of Princeton. She earned her bachelor's degree from Dillard University and her master's and doctorate from Harvard in Romance languages and literatures. The president of France named her chevalier of the French Legion of Honor, and President Biden named her to the White House HBCU Advisory Board.

To inquire about booking Ruth Simmons for a speaking engagement, please contact the Penguin Random House Speakers Bureau at speakers@penguinrandomhouse.com.

ABOUT THE TYPE

This book was set in Fairfield, the first typeface from the hand of the distinguished American artist and engraver Rudolph Ruzicka (1883–1978). Ruzicka was born in Bohemia (in the present-day Czech Republic) and came to America in 1894. He set up his own shop, devoted to wood engraving and printing, in New York in 1913 after a varied career working as a wood engraver, in photoengraving and banknote printing plants, and as an art director and freelance artist. He designed and illustrated many books, and was the creator of a considerable list of individual prints—wood engravings, line engravings on copper, and aquatints.